This Language, A River
Workbook

D1708103

This Language, A River

A HISTORY OF ENGLISH

WORKBOOK

K. AARON SMITH AND SUSAN M. KIM

broadview press

BROADVIEW PRESS – www.broadviewpress.com
Peterborough, Ontario, Canada

Founded in 1985, Broadview Press remains a wholly independent publishing house. Broadview's focus is on academic publishing; our titles are accessible to university and college students as well as scholars and general readers. With 800 titles in print, Broadview has become a leading international publisher in the humanities, with world-wide distribution. Broadview is committed to environmentally responsible publishing and fair business practices.

© 2020 K. Aaron Smith and Susan M. Kim

All rights reserved. No part of this book may be reproduced, kept in an information storage and retrieval system, or transmitted in any form or by any means, electronic or mechanical, including photocopying, recording, or otherwise, except as expressly permitted by the applicable copyright laws or through written permission from the publisher.

Library and Archives Canada Cataloguing in Publication

Title: This language, a river : a history of language : workbook / K. Aaron Smith and Susan M. Kim.
Names: Smith, K. Aaron (Kelly Aaron), 1965- author. | Kim, Susan M., author. | Supplement to (work):
    Smith, K. Aaron (Kelly Aaron), 1965- This language, a river.
Identifiers: Canadiana (print) 20200207741 | Canadiana (ebook) 20200207776 | ISBN 9781554814527
    (softcover) | ISBN 9781770487383 (PDF) | ISBN 9781460406946 (EPUB)
Subjects: LCSH: English language—History—Problems, exercises, etc. | LCGFT: Problems and exercises.
Classification: LCC PE1075 .S65 2020 Suppl. | DDC 420.9—dc23

Broadview Press handles its own distribution in North America:
PO Box 1243, Peterborough, Ontario K9J 7H5, Canada
555 Riverwalk Parkway, Tonawanda, NY 14150, USA
Tel: (705) 743-8990; Fax: (705) 743-8353
email: customerservice@broadviewpress.com

For all territories outside of North America, distribution is handled by Eurospan Group.

Broadview Press acknowledges the financial support of the Government of Canada for our publishing activities.

Canada

Edited by Martin R. Boyne

Book design by Chris Rowat Design

PRINTED IN CANADA

*As always, our teaching of the history of English is inspired
and made better by our students, and it is to them
that we dedicate this workbook.*

Contents

Preface

This workbook has been written as an accompaniment to our textbook, *This Language, A River*. The chapters of the workbook correspond to chapters of the textbook and are intended to expand, enlarge, and refine the material therein. As readers will notice, the exercises in the workbook are graded into beginning, intermediate, and advanced groupings, which will aid in making the textbook appropriate for different levels of students, from beginning to advanced undergraduates, and for introductory graduate courses on the history of English. Readers will also notice that we often return to certain topics in the intermediate and advanced sections of the exercises with increased difficulty/challenge. Most exercises include examples, and full answers to the exercises can be found in the Answer Key at the end of the workbook. The authors are happy to correspond with users of the textbook and workbook by email at kasmit3@ilstu.edu and/or smkim2@ilstu.edu.

Chapter One

1-1. Synchrony and Diachrony

Identify the following synchronic or diachronic statements. The first is completed for you as an example.

A. *Synchronic* In 1964, the Warren Commission submitted its report on the assassination of President Kennedy to then-president Lyndon B. Johnson.

B. _____ This morning I had avocado toast for breakfast.

C. _____ Yesterday I had avocado toast for breakfast.

D. _____ Two years ago I had never heard of avocado toast, but now that I live with two millennials, I have avocado toast for breakfast regularly.

E. _____ In Old English, the word for "bridegroom" was *brydguma*, a compound made up of the word for "bride" and a word meaning "man."

F. _____ In Early Modern English, speakers used the similar element *grome*, meaning "boy" or "lad," in the compound *brydguma*, producing *brydgrome*.

G. _____ Although it may be tempting to conjecture that the word "bridegroom" has something to do with the role of grooming in weddings, or with some notion that the husband to be is supposed to be serving as a groom to the bride, the word "bridegroom" comes into Modern English after the substitution (in the Early Modern period) of the element *grome* when the original Old English word *guma* had been lost.

H. _____ Even in the early part of the twentieth century, operagoers distinguished between the forms *brava* and *bravo*: *brava* was exclaimed after a performance by a female singer, and *bravo* was exclaimed after a performance by a male singer.

I. _____ At the present time, many operagoers simply use one form, *bravo*, when they are shouting their approval for a performance.

J. _____ "It would be a brave person who would follow Fowler's advice (1926) to use *bravo* when applauding a male singer in an operatic performance, *brava* for a female singer, and *bravi* for the company. Gender and number distinctions have been abandoned in such circumstances and *bravo* is the only cry of the three heard in English theaters now." (R.W. Burchfield, ed., *The New Fowler's Modern English Usage*, Clarendon Press, 1996.)

1-2. Internal and External

Imagine that you have, for some reason, been isolated on an island with a group of other English speakers. Don't worry, you will be rescued and make millions from writing about your adventures later. But you do remain on The Island for years. During the time on The Island, the following changes take place in your language. Identify those changes as internally or externally motivated. The first is completed for you as an example.

A. *Internal* Members of the Island community use the word *hope* a lot, since they spend much time talking about what they wish would happen. After some time, members of the Island group begin saying "hope" at the beginning of a sentence that is not true but instead expresses a hope or desire on the part of the speaker.

B. _____ There is a very attractive and charismatic leader in the group in whose dialect the word *olive* is pronounced much as most speakers pronounce the word *alive*. Olives are a staple on The Island. By the end of your time there, you too pronounce the word in this way, as does everyone else in the group.

C. _____ There survived one copy of a game (and just enough battery power to play it for years) that involved slaying monsters. You get points each time you slay a monster. When you and your fellow Islanders get together to talk about the game, you start worrying whether to say "I slew" or "I slayed" however many monsters. You don't have any way of looking it up. You agree in the end that since most verbs in English make their past tense forms with *–ed*, you will go with *slayed* rather than *slew* as the past tense form.

D. _____ The verb *want* is used very frequently on The Island. Everyone wants to go home, wants to see their families again, wants to shower, etc. Increasingly, however, *want* starts to signal intention rather than solely desire. So *I want to fix the hammock* signals intention to fix the hammock. By the end of your time on The Island, speakers will use a very reduced form of *want to*, *anna*, as in *She anna fix the hammock*, in which *anna* is indicating not that the action is desired or intended but that the action will take place in the future.

E. _____ There was a brief period of contact with speakers of French, who stayed for about a year but then departed in the night. While they were there, they taught everyone great things to do with coconut. You all start to call coconut by the French expression *noix de coco* when you make tarts with it, and you use the French expression *huile de coco* for conditioner.

PART TWO: INTERMEDIATE EXERCISES

2-1. Synchrony and Diachrony

Link the following synchronic statements into diachronic statements. The first is completed for you as an example.

A. 1. In Old English, the verb *willan* chiefly expressed desire: "to want (something in the future)."

A. 2. In Middle and Modern English, desire was more often expressed by the verb *want*, and forms of *will* were used as an auxiliary verb to express futurity.

> *The Old English verb willan was replaced in Middle English by want as a means of expressing desire. Will, meanwhile, became an auxiliary verb used to express futurity.*

B. 1. Old English retained a pronoun called the dual from Germanic that referred to two and only two people.

B. 2. Middle English did not have a dual pronoun.

C. 1. In Middle English there was a construction for indicating the place where something was occurring. It was made up of *on* with an *–ing* form: *The king is on hunting* meant *The king is in the forest (where he is hunting)*.

C. 2. In Early Modern English (EModE) the *on* in *The king is on hunting* had reduced to *a-*, as in *The king is a-hunting*, in answer to both the question "Where is the king?" and the question "What is the king doing?"

2-2. Internally and Externally Motivated Changes

The following are statements of some of the internal and external motivations for change in the history of English. You will have the opportunity to explore both the motivations and the changes that actually occurred in the course of reading the textbook. Here we ask you to consider a motivation and what might be its likely outcomes. In the history of a language, we can never predict exactly what will occur, but we can suggest what might be likely, given what happens in the histories of languages around the world. Nonetheless, you can check your predictions here with the discussions in the textbook of what actually occurred.

How do you predict that the following situations might change the language? The first is completed for you as an example.

A. During the colonial period, English speakers increasingly came into contact with indigenous languages in the Americas, Asia, Africa, and Pacific Islands. Those languages already had words for the many new kinds of plants and animals that the English speakers learned about in these areas.

> *It is likely that the English speakers, who were new to these areas, borrowed words from those indigenous languages for many of the plants and animals they encountered, like banyan tree or skunk.*

B. Words in Old English tended to be stressed on their first syllable. Much grammatical information was carried at the ends of words, in unstressed suffixes.

_____

_____

_____

_____

C. Latin is the language of the Church throughout the Middle Ages. Latin is used for all Church services, but also for much of the education that is conducted through the Church.

_____

_____

_____

_____

D. During the Early Modern period, speakers of English settled in places at quite a distance from England, for example in New England. Those settlers were geographically isolated from England but also sometimes intentionally separated politically and socially from the English communities they had left.

_____

_____

_____

_____

E. A rather large population of speakers of Old Norse and speakers of Old English lived in very close proximity in England during the Old English period. Old Norse and Old English are closely related languages, such that in some dialects, there might have been mutual intelligibility between them.

_____

_____

_____

_____

F. The most common way to make a noun plural, even in Old English which had many other ways to mark the plural, was to add a suffix with –s as part of it.

_____

_____

_____

_____

PART THREE: ADVANCED EXERCISES

3-1. Internally and Externally Motivated Changes

Although we separate internal and external motivations for language change for the purposes of organizing our presentation, we must recognize that these kinds of motivations cannot be wholly separable, and in most instances we can perceive a fairly complex interaction between the two in a given development.

The following questions should suggest to you more than one possible answer. As you sort out the different possibilities for the answer, see if you can identify the internal and external motivations for language change that inform your response.

1. What is the plural of *syllabus*?
    Why did you choose one or the other of the possibilities?

2. Does the phrase, as it occurs on signs near religious buildings at Easter time, *Christ is risen* mean the same thing as *Christ has risen*?
    What is the difference in meaning (if there is one)?

3. What does *ain't* mean, as in *He ain't home*? Is it legitimate to say that *ain't* isn't a word? Sometimes people justify that statement by claiming "*ain't* isn't in the dictionary." Is it in "the" dictionary? Is it in all dictionaries?

4. Does teen "slang" change faster than, say, Standard English? Why does it seem that some varieties of English change more quickly than others?

Notes

Chapter Two

1-1. Parts of Speech

Identify the part of speech of the underlined words in the following paragraph as a **noun**, **verb**, **adjective**, **adverb**, **preposition**, or **conjunction**. The first is completed for you as an example.

<u>During</u> the 17th Century, <u>England</u> and The United Provinces (the present-day
  (A)   (B)

Netherlands) <u>were</u> locked in a <u>fierce</u> competition on <u>several</u> fronts. On the one
         (C)   (D)   (E)

hand, the English <u>sought</u> to <u>develop</u> the <u>means</u> and methods of cloth-finishing at
            (F)   (G)   (H)

home, a <u>profitable</u> industry more <u>fully</u> developed in Leiden. As it stood <u>in</u> the early
      (I)   (J)   (K)

part of the century, English <u>cloth</u> would <u>be</u> only <u>partially</u> prepared <u>and</u> <u>then</u> <u>shipped</u>
                  (L)   (M)   (N)   (O) (P) (Q)

to Leiden <u>for</u> finishing. The English, seeking to increase <u>profit</u>, reasoned that if <u>raw</u>
      (R)   (S)   (T)

cloth was fully finished <u>domestically</u>, they could eliminate the Leiden middlemen,
                   (U)

but <u>ascendancy</u> in that market would not be so <u>easy</u>.
     (V)   (W)

(A) *Preposition*

(B) _____

(C) _____

(D) _____
(E) _____
(F) _____
(G) _____
(H) _____
(I) _____
(J) _____
(K) _____
(L) _____
(M) _____
(N) _____
(O) _____
(P) _____
(Q) _____
(R) _____
(S) _____
(T) _____
(U) _____
(V) _____
(W) _____

1-2. Noun Plurals

Give the plural of the following nouns. Which are regular and which are irregular? The first is completed for you as an example.

Singular	Plural	Regular or Irregular
A. deer	*deer*	*irregular*
B. sheep	_____	_____
C. man	_____	_____
D. eye	_____	_____
E. shoe	_____	_____
F. foot	_____	_____
G. knife	_____	_____
H. cup	_____	_____

I. mouse   _____   _____

J. brick   _____   _____

K. ox   _____   _____

1-3. Names of Verb Forms

One of the reasons to review grammar fundamentals when first embarking on study of the history of English is to ensure that we have a shared vocabulary for talking about language and language change. In this exercise, provide the names of the underlined verb forms in the following sentences taken from the chart given. The names in the chart correspond to the verb forms exemplified in Chapter Two of the textbook. The first is completed for you as an example.

Simple Present	Present Progressive	Present Perfect	Present Perfect Progressive
Simple Past	Past Progressive	Past Perfect	Past Perfect Progressive
Simple Future I	Simple Future I Progressive	Simple Future I Perfect	Simple Future I Perfect Progressive

A. The singer had left the building discreetly through a door in the back of the staging area before the screaming mob of fans discovered she was no longer there. *Past Perfect*

B. Najwana wrote in her diary every day until she began college.

   _____

C. My son will be living on campus for the first two years. After that, he has the option of choosing off-campus housing.

   _____

D. By next year, Frank will have been living in Seattle for three years already. How time flies!

   _____

E. Our family <u>goes</u> to a local farm every spring to pick blueberries.

_____

F. The hatchlings <u>were following</u> their mother across the road in single file while drivers waited.

_____

G. Charley <u>has been working</u> as a camp counselor since he was a teenager.

_____

H. Brigitte <u>had been working</u> in her garden when suddenly she heard an angry exchange coming from her neighbor's house.

_____

I. We <u>will do</u> our best, but frankly the odds seem stacked against us.

_____

J. I <u>am getting</u> better at tennis with lots of practice.

_____

K. Surely you already <u>will have heard</u> the warning, but in case you haven't, texting and driving is exceedingly dangerous.

_____

L. Zeph <u>has taken</u> two semesters of Latin and will begin his third semester in the fall.

_____

1-4. Comparative and Superlative Adjectives

Provide the comparative and superlative forms for the following adjectives. Take special note of those that take the inflection -er/-est and those that are modified by the adverbs *more/most*. You will recall from the textbook that the "basic" form of the adjective is called the "positive degree." The first is completed for you as an example.

Positive	Comparative	Superlative
A. large	*larger*	*largest*
B. big	_____	_____
C. atrocious	_____	_____
D. cold	_____	_____

E. remarkable   _____   _____

F. circular   _____   _____

G. long   _____   _____

H. warm   _____   _____

I. cute   _____   _____

J. obnoxious   _____   _____

K. sensitive   _____   _____

1-5. Noun Functions

Identify the function of the underlined nouns in the following sentences as **subject, direct object, indirect object, object of a preposition, subject complement,** or **object complement**. The first is completed for you as an example.

The older <u>woman</u> stood next to the waiting <u>van</u>.
        (A)   (B)

<u>Agamemnon</u> took his hot <u>coffee</u> from the second <u>counter</u>.
   (C)   (D)   (E)

The popular <u>designer</u> will show many eager <u>buyers</u> his new <u>collection</u> in the <u>summer</u>.
           (F)   (G)   (H)   (I)

<u>City Council</u> named the florist <u>shop</u> the best new <u>business</u> of 2019.
   (J)   (K)   (L)

<u>Darius</u> will be your knowledgeable <u>guide</u> this afternoon.
 (M)   (N)

The <u>light switch</u> for the <u>kitchen</u> is located on the <u>wall</u> above the <u>buffet</u>.
     (O)   (P)   (Q)   (R)

I offered <u>Elena</u> a free <u>ride</u> to her <u>work</u>.
      (S)   (T)   (U)

The antiquated <u>espresso machine</u> has been a decorative <u>fixture</u> in the <u>restaurant</u> for
            (V)   (W)   (X)
many years.

The <u>post office</u> can sell its <u>customers</u> <u>boxes</u> of many <u>sizes</u>.
     (Y)   (Z)   (AA)   (BB)

Our recent <u>graduates</u> will become the <u>leaders</u> of our <u>community</u> in the coming <u>years</u>.
     (CC)   (DD)   (EE)   (FF)

(A)   *Subject*

(B)   _____

(C)   _____

(D) _____

(E) _____

(F) _____

(G) _____

(H) _____

(I) _____

(J) _____

(K) _____

(L) _____

(M) _____

(N) _____

(O) _____

(P) _____

(Q) _____

(R) _____

(S) _____

(T) _____

(U) _____

(V) _____

(W) _____

(X) _____

(Y) _____

(Z) _____

(AA) _____

(BB) _____

(CC) _____

(DD) _____

(EE) _____

(FF) _____

PART TWO: INTERMEDIATE EXERCISES

2-1. Parts of Speech

Identify the part of speech of the underlined words in the following paragraph as **noun, lexical verb, auxiliary verb, adjective, adverb, preposition, coordinate conjunction, subordinate conjunction, personal pronoun, indefinite pronoun, possessive pronoun, possessive determiner, demonstrative determiner, definite article,** or **indefinite article**. The first is completed for you as an example.

The Gothic language is attested almost exclusively from fourth-century biblical
(A)   (B)   (C)   (D)   (E)
material translated from Greek and Latin sources. Structurally, Gothic is similar to
                                (F)   (G)   (H)
other Germanic languages, although some rather non-Germanic elements appear
(I)   (J)   (K)
in Gothic texts, undoubtedly linked to the morphology and syntax of those translation
                            (L)   (M)
sources. Historically, philologists at various times had placed Gothic in closer relation
(N)   (O)
to Northern Germanic or Western Germanic, but now it is more customary to regard
                              (P) (Q)
Gothic as comprising an Eastern branch, sharing certain of its features with both
                 (R) (S)   (T)   (U)
relational groups.

In terms of the geographical origin of the Goths, scholars are largely in agreement
                                    (V)
that they came from Scandinavia in the first century of the current era. That
(W) (X)   (Y)
Scandinavian origin has been known since the medieval period, an account
                (Z)   (AA)   (BB)
having been offered in Jordanes' 551 book, *De origine actibusque Getarum*. We can
                                               (CC)(DD)
assume that Jordanes' theory on the origins of the Goths is not his, but that he was
(EE) (FF)   (GG)   (HH)   (II)
transmitting information generally known to everyone at that time.
                              (JJ)   (KK)

(A)   *Definite Article*

(B)   _____

(C) _____

(D) _____

(E) _____

(F) _____

(G) _____

(H) _____

(I) _____

(J) _____

(K) _____

(L) _____

(M) _____

(N) _____

(O) _____

(P) _____

(Q) _____

(R) _____

(S) _____

(T) _____

(U) _____

(V) _____

(W) _____

(X) _____

(Y) _____

(Z) _____

(AA) _____

(BB) _____

(CC) _____

(DD) _____

(EE) _____

(FF) _____

(GG) _____

(HH) _____

(II) _____

(JJ) _____

(KK) _____

2-2. Parts of Speech

The words in the following list can represent at least two different parts of speech. For example, the word *walk* can be a noun, as in *We took a lovely walk*, or it can be a verb as in *We walk to school every day*. Identify two parts of speech categories for each word in the list below and write a sentence showing its use in each. You may add inflectional material to the word in your sample sentences; for example, you may make the word plural by adding *-s* or past tense by adding *-ed*, etc. In some cases a word may be used in more than two parts of speech categories. If you get stuck, you should consult a dictionary. The first is completed for you as an example.

		Part of Speech	Use
A. crush	1.	*noun*	*I have a crush on Rick Springfield.*
	2.	*verb*	*The wrecking ball crushed the concrete wall.*
B. up	1.	_____	_____
	2.	_____	_____
C. sign	1.	_____	_____
	2.	_____	_____
D. out	1.	_____	_____
	2.	_____	_____
E. level	1.	_____	_____
	2.	_____	_____
F. light	1.	_____	_____
	2.	_____	_____
G. chair	1.	_____	_____
	2.	_____	_____
H. best	1.	_____	_____
	2.	_____	_____
I. hound	1.	_____	_____
	2.	_____	_____
J. forward	1.	_____	_____
	2.	_____	_____

2-3. Noun Plurals

In exercise 1-2, you provided the plural for several nouns. It is likely that you had very little trouble determining the plural form for each of the nouns in that list. Provide the plurals for the words in the following list. Are you less certain about your decisions now? Why do you think that is?

Singular	Plural
A. syllabus	_____
B. hoof	_____
C. alumna	_____
D. addendum	_____
E. diagnosis	_____
F. appendix	_____
G. cactus	_____
H. half	_____
I. matrix	_____
J. wharf	_____

2-4. Pronoun and Determiner Forms

Provide the correct form of the pronoun or possessive determiner for the blank in each sentence. The first is completed for you as an example.

A. Nino took *them* to the concert and everyone enjoyed it entirely. (third person plural)

B. _____ students are circulating a petition to force the university to establish a committee to seek ways of lowering tuition. (first person plural)

C. My brother and _____ have been best friends since grammar school. (third person singular masculine)

D. _____ and your wife's anniversary falls on a Saturday this year, doesn't it? (second person singular)

E. The lawyer assured us that the matter would remain strictly between him and _____. (first person singular)

F. Both their son and _____ are eligible for significant tax rebates because of the new tax law. (third person plural)

G. Pouya's and _____ appointment is for next Wednesday at noon. (first person singular)

H. You can go in directly after _____. (third person singular feminine)

I. Don't forget to give Marsha or _____ your completed form before Friday. (first person plural)

J. _____ has been raining for several days and flooding is becoming a serious concern. (third person singular neuter)

2-5. Passive Forms

Turn the underlined active clauses into their passive counterparts. When doing so, make certain to keep the verb in the same tense/aspect category. For example, if the active verb is in the present perfect (*has seen*), make sure the passive verb stays in the present perfect form (*has been seen* not *was seen*). The first is completed for you as an example.

A. <u>The company replaced my cell phone</u> after it stopped working after only one week. *My cell phone was replaced (by the company)...*

B. <u>The driver has left your package on the back patio of your house</u>.

_____

C. <u>The guards were transferring the inmates to a new cell block</u> when the riot broke out.

_____

D. <u>The cook makes the dish with many ingredients</u> that can only be found in specialty shops.

_____

E. <u>Someone had erased the board</u> before the next class entered the room.

_____

F. <u>Researchers are compiling resources</u> so that the students can carry out their studies more efficiently.

_____

G. <u>The company has installed four new relay towers throughout the state.</u>

_____

2-6. Modal and Quasi-Modal Auxiliaries

Modal auxiliaries and quasi-modal expressions, in some cases, convey meanings such as permission, ability, necessity, obligation, and suggestion. First identify whether the modal meaning is expressed by a true modal verb or a quasi-modal expression in each of the sentences below. Then determine the modal meaning for each sentence. If more than one meaning is available, say so. The first is completed for you as an example.

A. The protesters <u>can</u> remain outside the property, but they are forbidden from entering the corporate grounds.

(Modal) or Quasi-Modal

Use: <u>permission</u>

B. When I was younger, I <u>could</u> easily stay up late. Now I'm lucky to be awake past nine!

Modal or Quasi-Modal

Use: _____

C. You <u>should</u> register your new espresso machine online. It will make it easier if you ever need to report a problem.

Modal or Quasi-Modal

Use: _____

D. No one <u>is allowed</u> in the park after nightfall, but of course everyone knows it's a popular hang-out for teens until midnight.

Modal or Quasi-Modal

Use: _____

E.   Charles <u>was supposed to</u> start college in the fall, but he suddenly decided to go backpacking across Europe instead!

Modal or Quasi-Modal

Use: _____

F.   You <u>might</u> take a different route because of the construction on Elm St. It's a real nightmare!

Modal or Quasi-Modal

Use: _____

G.   We <u>have to</u> arrange for a pet sitter before our trip in July.

Modal or Quasi-Modal

Use: _____

H.   Simon <u>ought to</u> help out more, but I'm afraid he has over-committed himself to too many activities, again!

Modal or Quasi-Modal

Use: _____

I.   I won't <u>be able to</u> come with you because of a previous engagement.

Modal or Quasi-Modal

Use: _____

J.   Hideki <u>must</u> count the money in the register every night and drop the deposit at the bank.

Modal or Quasi-Modal

Use: _____

K.   Customers <u>may</u> have a sample of any flavor.

Modal or Quasi-Modal

Use: _____

2-7. Comparative and Superlative Adjectives

In exercise 1-4, you provided the comparative and superlative forms for some adjectives. It is likely that you had little trouble deciding whether to use the inflectional -er/-est form or the adverbial *more/most* modification. In this exercise, there is a list of 10 more adjectives for which you should again provide the comparative and superlative forms. What you will probably find is that you will be less certain of the pattern to choose. What is different about these adjectives that makes their comparative and superlative forms less certain?

Positive	Comparative	Superlative
A. sunny	_____	_____
B. handsome	_____	_____
C. tender	_____	_____
D. lively	_____	_____
E. awesome	_____	_____
F. nimble	_____	_____
G. crappy	_____	_____
H. clever	_____	_____

2-8. Noun Functions

Identify the function of the underlined nouns in the following sentences as **subject, direct object, indirect object, object of a preposition, subject complement,** or **object complement.** The first is completed for you as an example.

After <u>Miguel</u> graduates, he plans to start his own <u>business</u>.
    (A)   (B)

Calling her best <u>friend</u> for confirmation, <u>Annie</u> took the <u>bet</u> over who had won the 1956
                        (C)   (D)   (E)
World Series.

Giving your <u>brother</u> a <u>gift</u> for his birthday would be a very kind <u>gesture</u>.
             (F)   (G)   (H)

The prize <u>committee</u> realized their <u>mistake</u> but only after having announced Deesha
              (I)   (J)
the <u>winner</u>.
   (K)

Yu-Min both wrote and performed the opening <u>piece</u> in the school <u>concert</u>.
  (L)   (M)   (N)

Becoming an <u>actor</u> at such a young <u>age</u>, <u>Miriam</u> lacked common <u>sense</u> and social
              (O)   (P) (Q)   (R)
<u>graces</u>.
  (S)

Before granting its <u>employees</u> any <u>awards</u>, the <u>company</u> performs a lengthy
                        (T)   (U)   (V)
<u>investigation</u> of all work-related <u>productivity</u> for each <u>member</u> of each <u>department</u>.
    (W)   (X)   (Y)   (Z)

His over-heated <u>computer</u> started to make a strange <u>noise</u>, so Ahmed closed the <u>screen</u>
             (AA)   (BB)   (CC)
and decided to take the <u>computer</u> to a repair <u>specialist</u>.
                (DD)   (EE)

Because of the <u>strike</u>, a <u>shortage</u> of newly manufactured automobile <u>parts</u> will likely be
          (FF)   (GG)   (HH)
the <u>outcome</u>.
   (II)

You may order hot or cold <u>drinks</u> at any <u>time</u> of the <u>year</u>, but we do not offer our full
                        (JJ)   (KK)   (LL)
<u>menu</u> from <u>May</u> to <u>September</u>.
(MM)   (NN)   (OO)

(A)   *Subject*

(B)   ————————————————

(C)   ————————————————

(D)   ————————————————

(E)   ————————————————

(F)   ————————————————

(G)   ————————————————

(H)   ————————————————

(I)   ————————————————

(J)   ————————————————

(K) _____

(L) _____

(M) _____

(N) _____

(O) _____

(P) _____

(Q) _____

(R) _____

(S) _____

(T) _____

(U) _____

(V) _____

(W) _____

(X) _____

(Y) _____

(Z) _____

(AA) _____

(BB) _____

(CC) _____

(DD) _____

(EE) _____

(FF) _____

(GG) _____

(HH) _____

(II) _____

(JJ) _____

(KK) _____

(LL) _____

(MM) _____

(NN) _____

(OO) _____

2-9. Sentence Types

Identify each of the sentences as **simple, compound, complex,** or **compound-complex,** according to the definitions given in Chapter Two of the textbook. The first is completed for you as an example.

A. A cup of coffee costs 2.50, but if you want a specialty coffee, the price varies.
    Compound-complex

B. Levi didn't contact the police or his insurance company after his minor accident.

    _____

C. Before she became a teacher, Alisha worked a variety of office support jobs.

    _____

D. Before turning on the car, you have to pull the wheel to the right to unlock the ignition switch.

    _____

E. We won't contribute any money to the fund nor will we attend any of the gatherings that such funds support.

    _____

F. Throughout the week, Selah either cooks or orders delivery from one of the many restaurants in her neighborhood.

    _____

G. A friend is someone who[1] you can look to for support in difficult times.

    _____

H. That the proposal was so unanimously supported attests to the skillful persuasive talent of its writer.

    _____

I. During the application process, Nicola frequently checked her status in the admissions websites at the several schools considering her application for admission to graduate school.

    _____

---

1 Since the relative pronoun here is the object of the preposition *to* in its own clause, one may select the form *whom. Whom* in such syntactic environments has become increasingly rare in most genres and registers of Present-day English. Here, as elsewhere in this workbook, we have chosen to follow the less formal variant.

2-10. Relative Pronoun Selection

Considering the relative pronouns **who/whom, that, which**, and zero, indicate which relative pronouns are possible in the blanks below. The first is completed for you as an example.

A. The tile *that, Ø* we put in the guest bathroom has already begun to peel from the wall.

B. I would have asked the woman _____ owns the hotel, if I had been you.

C. People are surprised to find out that I have never seen the original Stars Wars movie, _____ was released when I was in eighth grade.

D. Magdalena Sanchez, _____ directs the after-school program, is currently hiring mentors and tutors.

E. After the meet, Valentine apologized to the other player _____ he kicked during a scuttle for the ball.

F. There will be someone waiting to _____ you can give your payment.

G. We should ask Ophelia, _____ we can always trust completely.

H. Zack filled the cup _____ Alexa passed to him.

I. On the flight I read the biography of Norman Bates, about _____ I knew practically nothing.

J. Notices have been sent to the members _____ have neglected to pay their dues.

2-11. Noun Clause Function

As you learned in the book, noun clauses perform the same functions as nouns (and noun phrases). Most commonly they are the **subject**, **direct object**, **subject complement**, or **object of a preposition**. Identify the function of the underlined noun clauses in the following sentences. The first is completed for you as an example.

A. I don't know <u>whether Liv will show up</u>, but I suspect not.
Noun Clause Function: *Direct Object*

B. <u>That you have asked the question in the first place</u> indicates that you already know more than you think you do.
Noun Clause Function: _____

C. The cafe workers argued about <u>who would have to close the store on New Year's Eve</u>.
Noun Clause Function: _____

D. Students always question <u>if they have to know the material from the book for the final exam</u>.
Noun Clause Function: _____

E. The truth is <u>that you still have several opportunities to bring your grade up</u>, but you will need to apply yourself more.
Noun Clause Function: _____

F. <u>How Lysander found out about his surprise party</u> is a mystery to us.
Noun Clause Function: _____

G. We don't mind <u>that the post office raised the price of stamps</u>, but we will likely switch to an online payment option.
Noun Clause Function: _____

H. Hector became <u>what he said he never would</u>, an AARP member!
Noun Clause Function: _____

I. Contemplating <u>whether she should take the new position</u>, Arabella reflected on the many close relationships she had built among her current colleagues.
Noun Clause Function: _____

J. <u>Whether I decide to go or not</u> shouldn't affect your decision one way or another!
Noun Clause Function: _____

2-12. Adverbial Clauses

In Chapter Two of the textbook, you learned that adverb clauses express **time, concession, cause, place,** or **condition.** Identify the meaning of each of the underlined adverb clauses in the sentences below. If the meaning is ambiguous, state that ambiguity in your answer. The first is completed for you as an example.

A. <u>Before she finally gave her permission,</u> Sophia had remained stubbornly opposed to the idea of her son's going on an overnight trip with his friends.
Adverbial Meaning: *time*

B. <u>Although I am your best friend,</u> I cannot support you on this point.
Adverbial Meaning: _____

C. I came to this school <u>because they offered me a very good scholarship</u>.
   Adverbial Meaning: _____

D. <u>If you call the number on the box</u>, they can offer help in the assembly of the table.
   Adverbial Meaning: _____

E. Moussa remained a bachelor <u>until he was 25 and met the love of his life</u>.
   Adverbial Meaning: _____

F. <u>Since Susan had agreed to work on organizing the tournament</u>, she quickly found
   herself overwhelmed with tasks.
   Adverbial Meaning: _____

G. <u>Unless Maurice formally apologizes to the Dean</u>, the school will not let him
   return.
   Adverbial Meaning: _____

H. A faithful pet will follow you <u>wherever you go</u>.
   Adverbial Meaning: _____

I. It won't be long now <u>before the results are made known to everyone</u>.
   Adverbial Meaning: _____

PART THREE: ADVANCED EXERCISES

3-1. Passive Verb Forms

In exercise 2-5, you transformed active clauses into passive ones. In that exercise, all of the verbs were simple transitives, meaning that they each had only one object and so the transformations were straightforward as you made that object into the subject of the passive verb. In this exercise, the verbs are ditransitive, meaning that they have two objects, a direct object and an indirect object. Transform each sentence into its passive counterpart in two ways, the first by making the indirect object into the subject and the second by making the direct object into the subject.

A. <u>Mr. Suzuki reads children traditional fairy tales every Saturday in the library</u>.

The children are read fairy tales (by Mr. Suzuki) every Saturday in the library.

Fairy tales are read to the children (by Mr. Suzuki) every Saturday in the library.

B. <u>The election committee did not show the public the recount numbers</u> until the results were firm.

_____

_____

_____

_____

C. <u>The theater has sold us the wrong tickets</u> even though I repeated the order twice.

_____

_____

_____

_____

D. <u>The human resources department will provide each retiree a comprehensive package</u> during the first week of his or her retirement.

_____

_____

_____

_____

E. <u>The welcoming committee should present all of the delegates a welcome in their own language.</u>

_____

_____

_____

F. <u>Gabor delivered the office all of the items ordered</u> but the office manager forgot to sign the invoice.

_____

_____

_____

G. <u>The President had been telling his cabinet lies</u> since the beginning of his term.[2]

_____

_____

_____

H. <u>The children handed Mrs. McGillicuddy the essays</u> at the end of the week.

_____

_____

_____

I. <u>Logan should pass Mia the ball</u> because she has an opening for a perfect shot.

_____

_____

_____

---

2 In this case the longer *had been being told* would be replaced by the shorter and stylistically more elegant *had been told*, as noted in the textbook Chapter Two.

3-2. Epistemic Modality

In addition to the kinds of meanings expressed in exercise 2-6, modal auxiliaries also have so-called epistemic meanings which express the speaker's/writer's certainty about what he/she is saying. Arrange the following sentences from most certain to least certain and compare your ranking with others in the class. How closely do you agree? Which modals show the most and least agreement?

(Upon hearing a knock on the door...)

That could be Florio.
That should be Florio.
That will be Florio.
That might be Florio.
That would be Florio.
That may be Florio.
That must be Florio.

Most certain: _____

   _____

   _____

   _____

   _____

   _____

Least certain: _____

3-3. Comparative and Superlative Adjectives

Consider the one- and two-syllable adjectives in the following list. Determine whether the adjectives sound acceptable or not with the *-er/-est* inflection. Compare your answers to those of your classmates. Can you discern a pattern among those adjectives for which *-er/-est* is unobjectionable and those for which the endings sound problematic? (Hint: you may want to look at the origin of the words in the *Oxford English Dictionary*.)

A. beige   beiger   beigest
B. slender   slenderer   slenderest
C. macho   machoer   machoest
D. fond   fonder   fondest
E. dire   direr   direst

F. brittle   brittler   brittlest
G. alto   altoer   altoest
H. frumpy   frumpier   frumpiest
I. moot   mooter   mootest
J. orange   oranger   orangest

3-4. Compounds

The word classes of noun and adjective can sometimes be difficult to distinguish in compounds, like *cover song* (noun + noun) and *high chair* (adjective + noun). However, we can note that *cover*, even though it functions to modify another noun, is still a noun. We know so because *cover* still does those things that nouns do: it can occur with a determiner, *the cover*; and it can be made plural, *covers*. Similarly the adjective *high* still acts like an adjective in that it can be made comparative or superlative: *high~higher~highest*. Consider the following list of compounds and determine whether the first element is a noun or an adjective. The first is completed for you as an example.

A. slow motion
   slow: *adjective*

B. ice cap
   ice: _____

C. window cover
   window: _____

D. desert rain
   desert: _____

E. rock bottom
   rock: _____

F. steel mill
   steel: _____

G. blackbird
   black: _____

H. quicksand
   quick: _____

I.   paper towel
     paper: _____

J.   late show
     late: _____

3-5. Relative Pronoun Function

Identify the relative pronoun in the following sentences and determine its syntactic function as the **subject**, **direct object**, or **object of a preposition**. Be aware that sometimes the relative pronoun has been omitted. In that case, say what the function of the relative pronoun was before it was omitted. The first is completed for you as an example.

A. The diners who requested to see the manager were angered by the waiter's rude behavior.
    The relative pronoun 'who' is functioning as the subject of its clause.

B. The city converted the park the children played in into a commercial area.
    _____

C. The group's new album, which debuted on an internet song-sharing site, is probably their best so far.
    _____

D. Charly Harper, who we studied in my art class, was an American naturalist artist.
    _____

E. You should consult the protocol manual in which the proper reporting structure for such matters may be found.
    _____

F. The clerk dressed the mannequin that the advertising department sent to him.
    _____

G. The public remain quite untrusting of automobiles that can drive themselves on public roads.
    _____

H. You can donate any article of clothing you no longer want.
    _____

I.   We never lock the door that you just came through.

_____

J.   I forgot several of the items you mentioned when I made our shopping list.

_____

K.   I forgot who you were talking about last night.

_____

3-6. Noun Clauses

Combine the following sentences by turning the first sentence into a noun clause and replacing the demonstrative in the second sentence with it. The first is completed for you as an example.

A.   Where did Alan finish his degree?
     His resume did not clearly indicate **this**.
     His resume did not clearly indicate where Alan finished his degree.

B.   Are the cookies ready?
     The child asked **this**.

_____

C.   Our car gets approximately 40 miles to a gallon of gas.
     This will save us several hundreds of dollars each year.

_____

D.   Where would the capitol be located?
     The founders of the new country debated **this**.

_____

E.   The television had been moved from its usual position.
     Song-Ha saw **this**.

_____

F.   The second edition of the book had been released.
     This necessitated a change in the cataloguing system.

_____

G. Aaron played his flute on the patio before dinner.
Moriki enjoyed **this**.

_____

H. When is the first day of class?
The students wondered about **this**. (Note that you may remove the preposition "about" when combining these sentences.)

_____

I. Does the city collect yard debris on Tuesdays?
No one is quite certain about **this**. (Note that you may remove the preposition "about" when combining these sentences.)

_____

J. They were only given two days to read the entire novel.
The students didn't like **this**.

_____

K. Did the coffee shop raise its prices after Christmas?
Kollandra asked me **this**.

_____

Notes

_____

_____

_____

_____

_____

_____

_____

_____

_____

_____

_____

_____

_____

_____

_____

_____

_____

_____

_____

_____

_____

_____

_____

_____

_____

_____

Chapter Three

1-1. Map

Fill in the following political map of present-day Europe.

1-2. Linguistic Reconstruction

In the textbook, you learned that it was Sir William Jones who noticed systematic similarities among some of the oldest languages in Europe and Asia and that the similarities were too striking to have occurred by accident. Consequently, he posited that those languages likely developed out of a shared ancestor language, which he proposed might no longer exist. In the years subsequent to Jones's observation, scholars have attempted to reconstruct this ancestral language (known as Proto-Indo-European) by comparing the correspondences of sounds in related words in those languages thought to have descended from it. In this exercise, you will have the opportunity to experience that striking similarity and to perform a simple reconstruction of Proto-Indo-European. Consider the list of related words in Latin, Greek, and Sanskrit. Based on the correspondences of consonants, what would you posit as the missing consonant in the parent Proto-Indo-European language? The first is completed for you as an example.

	Latin	Greek	Sanskrit		PIE
A.	decem[1]	deka	dasha	'ten'	d e k mt
B.	ped-	pod-	pada	'foot'	____ o ____ s
C.	tres	tres	treeni	'three'	____ reye ____
D.	nepot-	nepod-	napat-	'grandson'	____ e ____ o ____
E.	mater	meter	matar	'mother'	____ e ____ e ____

1-3. Borrowing

It is highly infrequent that native words end in -o in English. However, there are a handful of words borrowed from other languages into English that do end in -o. Consider the following list of words in English. What language do you think they come from? What do you believe to be the general circumstances of their borrowing? That is, why do you think they were borrowed? (You may want to consult the *Oxford English Dictionary* to check on the language of origin and meaning of some of the words.)

A. gumbo   _____

B. calico   _____

C. ouzo   _____

D. piano   _____

E. arpeggio   _____

F. ex officio   _____

G. taboo   _____

---

1   Latin <c> is [k] phonetically.

1-4. Cognates

Consider the following list of words shared between English and other languages. Do you believe the words are cognates (words co-developed from the parent language)? Or do you believe the similarity reflects borrowing? Why do you think so? If it is a borrowing, what is the direction of borrowing, from English or into English? You may want to confirm your sense of the direction of the borrowing by consulting the etymological information in the *Oxford English Dictionary*. The first is completed for you as an example.

A. English: door   Dutch: deur

These seem to be cognates since Dutch and English descend from the same parent language and share a lot of core vocabulary.

B. English: honcho   Japanese: hancho

_____

_____

C. English: hair   German: Haar

_____

_____

D. English: baby   Chinese: běibí

_____

_____

E. English: lips   Spanish: labios

_____

_____

F. English: shish kebab   Turkish: şiş kebabı

_____

_____

G. English: cherub   Hebrew: cherub

_____

_____

H. English: brother   Russian: brat

_____

_____

I. English: eight   Bengali: aat

_____

_____

J. English: squash   Narragansett: askútasquash

_____

_____

1-5. Doublets

The term "doublet" refers to related words that have been borrowed twice from the same language, albeit at different times and under different social conditions. Consider the list of five doublets borrowed into English from Latin (sometimes via French) and look them up in the *Oxford English Dictionary*. Which are older borrowings and which are more recent? Are there any characteristics of the words in terms of their meanings or forms that distinguish the two groups generally?

A. frail   fragile

_____

B. crown   coronation

_____

C. delight   delectable

_____

D. dainty   dignity

_____

E. school   scholastic

_____

1-6. Indo-European

Fill in the blanks in the following diagram of the Indo-European languages with languages that would fit into the subfamily indicated.

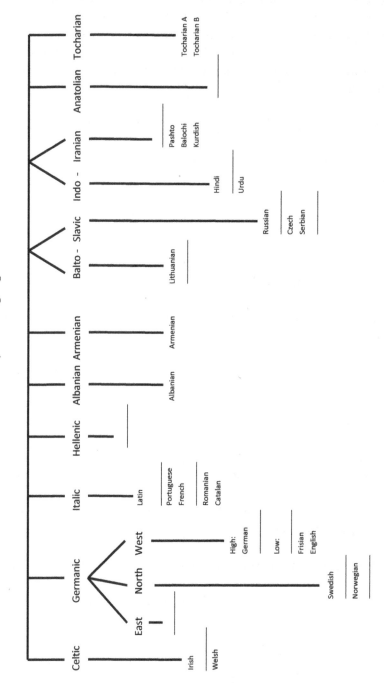

1-7. Case

In Chapter Three of the textbook, case is defined as a "system in which a noun or pronoun…changes form according to whether it is being used as the subject, direct object, indirect object, object of a preposition, etc." In order to get a better sense of how case works, consider the sentences below in which each Noun (Noun Phrase) is followed by a blank. In each blank, place an **X** if the Noun (Noun Phrase) functions as a subject or a subject complement, an **O** if it is a direct object or an object complement, **A** for indirect object, and **P** for object of a preposition. The first is completed for you as an example.

A. The excited students __X__ showed their parents __A__ the brochure __O__ .

B. In 1476, William Caxton _____ introduced the moveable-type printing press _____ to England _____.

C. The old apple tree _____ was cut down by the farmer _____ and its wood _____ was burned in the fire place _____ during that winter _____.

D. After the town parade _____, the marching band _____ held a recital _____ in the school gym _____.

E. The voters _____ from our neighboring town _____ have elected Alexandra Lidell _____ mayor _____.

F. Honesty _____ truly is the best policy _____ in nearly every situation _____, but sometimes a person _____ is better to simply stay quiet.

G. Hand Amaria _____ the book _____ from the shelf _____.

H. The post office _____ is the place _____ where young people can register for the draft _____.

I. My mother _____ always kept her shopping list _____ on the refrigerator door _____ next to photos _____ of our vacations _____.

J. The Council _____ has named your band _____ the best act _____ of 2018.

K. My sister _____ sent me _____ a picture _____ of her cat _____.

PART TWO: INTERMEDIATE EXERCISES

2-1. Geography and Indo-European Languages

In the beginning section of exercises for this chapter, you were asked to identify countries in modern-day Europe to familiarize yourself with the geography of some of the areas in which Indo-European languages are spoken. However, the geography of Indo-European languages stretches well into the Middle East and Central Asia, at least historically. For this exercise, identify the countries indicated on the following map. Then, consult the website Ethnologue (www.ethnologue. com) and list the Indo-European languages (or at least some of them) spoken in those countries.

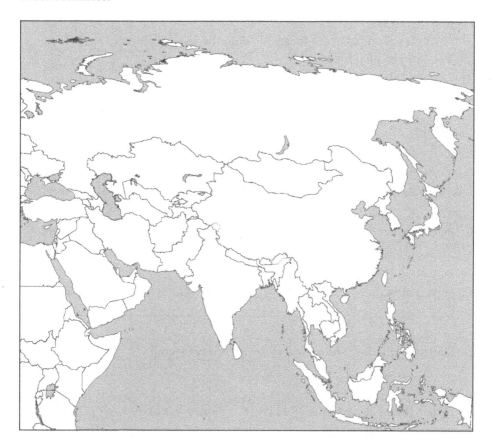

2-2. Cognates

The following list shows a set of cognates in Spanish, Portuguese, and Italian, three languages we know to have descended from Latin. In fact, those three languages as well as the other Romance languages did not develop directly from Latin but instead developed from Vulgar Latin, that is, the variety of spoken Latin used by everyday people (including soldiers and merchants throughout the Roman Empire) during the first three centuries CE. For each of the sets of cognates, the presumed Vulgar Latin word is given. State the changes that you observe for the set of words in each line. What language(s) shows a change? What exactly is that change? Do the changes you observe occur in other word sets too? Can you make a generalization about certain of the changes in sounds from Vulgar Latin to Spanish, Portuguese, or Italian? Broad phonetic transcriptions are provided in order to track the details of the changes involved. Make note of the following phonetic symbols. Note that you may want to return to this exercise after learning phonetics in Chapter Four of the textbook. The first is completed for you as an example.

Phonetic Symbols:
[ɾ] is a single voiced tap of the tongue tip onto the alveolar ridge
[β] is a voiced bilabial fricative
[r] is a voiced alveolar trill
[ɲ] is a voiced palatal nasal (compare the letter <ñ> in Spanish)

Spanish	Portuguese	Italian	Vulgar Latin
A. harina [aɾina]	farina [faɾina]	farina [faɾina]	farina [faɾina]

The beginning [f] of Vulgar Latin appears to have been deleted in Spanish.

Spanish	Portuguese	Italian	Vulgar Latin
B. pluma [pluma]	pluma [pluma]	piuma [pjuma]	pluma [pluma]
C. cubo [kuβo]	cubo [kubu]	cubo [kubo]	cubo [kubo]
D. haber [aβer]	haver [aver]	avere [avere]	habere [habere]
E. blanco [blanko]	blanco [blanku]	bianco [bjanko]	blanco [blanko]
F. caminar [kaminaɾ]	caminhar [kamiɲar]	camminare [kamminare]	caminare [kaminare]

G. casa [kasa]   casa [kaza]   casa [kaza]   casa [kasa]

H. cosa [kosa]   coisa [koiza]   cosa [koza]   cosa [kosa]

I. tierra [tjera]   terra [tera]   terra [tera]   terra [tera]

J. piedra [pjedra]   pedra [pedra]   pietra [pjetra]   petra [petra]

2-3. Cognates

Consider the following cognates (related words in separate languages) that are common to several Polynesian languages, among them Tongan, Hawaiian, and Samoan. After studying the words answer the questions that follow.

	Tongan	Hawaiian	Samoan
'flower'	siale	kiele	tiale
'canoe'	vaka	wa'a	va'a
'sand'	one'one	one	oneone
'woman'	fafina	wahine	fafina
'man'	tangata	kanaka	tagata

Note: <'> represents a glottal stop [?] in the orthography of these languages.

A. How would you characterize these cognates in terms of their meanings?

B. Why are these words common to all three languages?

C. What words would you expect NOT to find commonly in these languages?

2-4. Borrowing

In exercise 1-4, you were presented with some words borrowed into English from various languages. It is likely that you found some of those borrowings to be culturally situated, that is, words borrowed along with a culturally foreign object or notion, like *shish kebab*. In fact, it is likely that you can still feel a level of foreignness in the borrowed term, in many cases.

For this exercise, you are again presented with a list of borrowings into English from other languages. Using a dictionary with etymological information (e.g., the *Oxford English Dictionary*), determine the source language for each and then consider the questions that follow the list.

                Origin

A. position   _____

B. cheese   _____

C. dinosaur   _____

D. skin   _____

E. ill   _____

F. balcony   _____

G. enthusiasm   _____

How would you characterize the differences between the words in this group and those in 1-4?

_____

_____

What do you think accounts for those differences?

_____

_____

2-5. Etymology

An important point made in Chapter Three of the textbook is that words may come into a language through retention from an earlier stage of the language, or they may be borrowed into a language from a foreign source. However, the origin of some words in a language can be rather messy. In some cases, we cannot determine whether a word is borrowed or native, and in other cases, part of a word may be borrowed and the other part native!

In this exercise, you are presented with words whose etymologies are messy. After consulting a dictionary with etymological information, like the *Oxford English Dictionary*, discuss the origins of the following words and how their etymologies are complex.

A. with

_____

B. teleprompter

_____

C. rich

_____

D. gain

_____

E. courtship

_____

2-6. Doublets

The following is a list of doublets (see exercise 1-5 from this chapter) in Spanish. Determine which you believe to be an older borrowing and which a more recent borrowing. Explain your answers by considering both the form of the words and their meanings. (You may confirm your hunches by consulting a Spanish dictionary with etymological information.)

Latin	A Spanish	B Spanish
A. cathedra 'seat'	cathedra 'a university professorship/chair'	cadera 'hip'

_____

_____

_____

B. capit- 'head'	capítulo 'chapter'	cabeza 'head'

_____

_____

_____

C. terra 'land'   territorio 'territory'   tierra 'land'

_____

_____

_____

D. ped- 'foot'   pedestal 'pedestal'   pie 'foot'

_____

_____

_____

E. auris 'ear'   auricular 'earpiece'   oreja 'ear'

_____

_____

_____

F. apiculu- 'bee [diminutive]'   apicultura 'bee-keeping'   abeja 'bee'

_____

_____

_____

G. mensa 'month'   mensual 'monthly'   mes 'month'

_____

_____

_____

PART THREE: ADVANCED EXERCISES

3-1. Indo-European Tree

Create your own Indo-European tree and feel free to be as creative as you like. You can perform an image search on Google for "Indo-European Tree" to get some ideas.

3-2. Geography and Indo-European Languages

In the first and second sections of exercises for this chapter, you were asked to identify countries in modern-day Europe and Asia where Indo-European languages are spoken. For this exercise, identify the countries around the world in which Indo-European languages are spoken. You may want to consult the website Ethnologue (www.ethnologue.com) in order to fill out the map. (In some instances, it may be difficult to determine the degree to which an Indo-European language is spoken, particularly in a colonial setting. For instance, English is certainly spoken in Nigeria as an administrative language, but the population generally speak various African languages as their first language. Chapter Ten of the textbook looks more closely at the global dimensions of English in countries like Nigeria.)

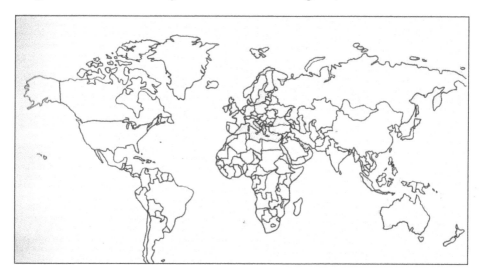

3-3. Cognates and Reconstruction

Consider the following cognate sets in Germanic. For each set, what would you suggest is a likely Proto-Germanic form, considering what you see here? (Obviously the set is quite limited and there may be more information necessary for a full reconstruction.) Which language appears to have made a change that the others didn't? How would you describe that change in phonetic terms? Note that you may want to return to this exercise after learning phonetics in Chapter Four of the textbook.

A. **German**   **Norse**   **Gothic**   **English**
   Fünf [fynf]   fimm [fɪm]   fimf [fɪmf]   five [fɑɪv]

B. **Dutch**   **English**   **Norwegian**   **German**
   Hopen [hopen]   hope [hop]   håpe [hop]   hoffen [hofen]

C. **German**   **English**   **Frisian**   **Icelandic**
   Zahn [tsɑn]   tooth [tuθ]   tosk [tosk]   tönn [tœn]

(note z = [ts] in German, and ö = œ in Icelandic, which is like pronouncing the
letter <a> and rounding your lips)

D. **Dutch**   **Norse**   **Norwegian**   **German**
   Ik [ɪk]   Ik [ɪk]   jeg [jaɪ]   ich [ɪç]

Notes

Notes

Chapter Four

1-1. Phonetics

The words in the right-hand column **begin** with sounds described in the left-hand column. Match the sounds to the descriptions. The first is completed for you as an example.

1. voiced, alveopalatal, affricate	A. character	5
2. voiceless, bilabial, stop	B. jar	_____
3. voiceless, interdental, fricative	C. happen	_____
4. voiced, labiodental, fricative	D. police	_____
5. voiceless, velar, stop	E. theme	_____
6. voiceless, glottal, fricative	F. yearbook	_____
7. voiced, palatal, approximant	G. bargain	_____
8. voiced, alveolar, central liquid	H. then	_____
9. voiced, bilabial, stop	I. renegade	_____
10. voiced, interdental, fricative	J. victory	_____

1-2. Phonetics

The words in the right-hand column **end** with sounds described in the left-hand column. Match the sounds to the descriptions. The first is completed for you as an example.

1. voiced, velar, nasal	A. cookies	6
2. voiced, interdental, fricative	B. swimming	_____

3. voiceless, labiodental, fricative	C. teeth	_____
4. voiceless, velar, stop	D. carafe	_____
5. voiced, alveolar, lateral liquid	E. relish	_____
6. voiced, alveolar, fricative	F. compel	_____
7. voiceless, alveolar, fricative	G. pulled	_____
8. voiceless, alveopalatal, fricative	H. breathe	_____
9. voiced, alveolar, stop	I. price	_____
10. voiceless, interdental, fricative	J. automatic	_____

1-3. Phonetics

The words in the right-hand column have their middle consonant sound described in the left-hand column. Match the sounds to the descriptions. The first is completed for you as an example.

1. voiced, bilabial, approximant	A. reaper	5
2. voiced, alveolar, fricative	B. assure	_____
3. voiced, bilabial, stop	C. aware	_____
4. voiced, velar, stop	D. buffer	_____
5. voiceless, bilabial, stop	E. either	_____
6. voiced, interdental, fricative	F. lemming	_____
7. voiceless, labiodental, fricative	G. fiber	_____
8. voiced, palatal, approximant	H. layer	_____
9. voiced, bilabial, nasal	I. sugar	_____
10. voiceless, alveopalatal, fricative	J. scissors	_____

1-4. Phonetics: Vowels

Identify the vowel in the underlined syllable using the IPA phonetic symbols from the textbook. Be sure to consider diphthongs when making your determination. The first is completed for you as an example.

A. <u>ra</u>dical   [æ]

B. il<u>lus</u>ion   _____

C. a<u>but</u>   _____

D. em<u>broi</u>dery   _____

E. hand<u>book</u>   _____

F. de<u>light</u>   _____

G. to<u>po</u>graphy   _____

H. de<u>bate</u>   _____

I. <u>e</u>steem   _____

J. ba<u>roque</u>   _____

K. be<u>cause</u>   _____

L. Ameri<u>ca</u>   _____

M. de<u>bris</u>   _____

N. a<u>rouse</u>   _____

O. <u>ri</u>dicule   _____

1-5. Reading Phonetics

Provide the English word for each of the phonetically-spelled items in the list below. The first is completed for you as an example.

A. [ɹɪtʃ]   *rich*

B. [pɛn]   _____

C. [θɪŋk]   _____

D. [ɛvɹi]   _____

E. [læʃ]   _____

F. [lʊk]   _____

G. [smok]   _____

H. [fil]   _____

I. [ɹæk]   _____

J. [kʌt]   _____

K. [tek]   _____

L. [ʃut]   _____

M. [əstaundɪŋ]   _____

N. [ɹili]   _____

O. [tɔt]   _____

P. [kɹev]   _____

Q. [ʃɛd]   _____

R. [ədʒʌst]   _____

S. [kedʒ]   _____

T. [saidɪŋ]   _____

1-6. Writing in Phonetics

Transcribe each of the following English words into phonetic spellings. The first is completed for you as an example.

A. sat   [sæt]

B. make   _____

C. fall   _____

D. rush   _____

E. cheap   _____

F. left   _____

G. brood   _____

H. put   _____

I. drive   _____

J. louse   _____

K. tight   _____

L. fuel   _____

M. joy   _____

N. base   _____

O. wood   _____

P. awake   _____

Q. between   _____

R. flood   _____

S. syntax   _____

T. city   _____

PART TWO: INTERMEDIATE EXERCISES

2-1. Working with /r/[1]

Vowels followed by /r/ in the same syllable are difficult to discern phonetically because there is a degree of overlap between the vowel and /r/. The effect of a following /r/ may place a vowel outside of its normal area of articulation. For example, the word *beer* may be produced with the vowel [i] followed by [ɹ], but only in very careful and somewhat strained pronunciation. *Beer* may also be pronounced with [ɪ] followed by [ɹ] in familiar, casual, or rapid speech. Probably for many American English speakers, the vowel in *beer* usually falls somewhere between [i] and [ɪ] in most speech situations.

Some phoneticians even talk of "/r/-coloring" on the vowel, and there is a special mark in IPA to indicate such "coloring," also known more generally as "rhoticity." For example, an /r/-colored schwa, which you hear at the end of a word like *maker* in American English, has the special symbol [ɚ]. Like all schwas in English, an /r/-colored schwa will appear in unstressed syllables, usually at the end of a word and commonly spelled <-er>. Some phoneticians will make a distinction between the r-colored vowel [ɝ] in stressed syllables, as in *bird*, as pronounced in Standard American English, and [ɚ] in unstressed syllables. Other than in the symbols [ɝ] and [ɚ], it is not common to use the rhoticity marker on vowels for transcribing English.

Transcribe the following words containing a vowel followed by /r/. Be prepared for much debate on the nature of the vowel. Use [ɝ] and [ɚ] in accordance with the explanation given above. The first is completed for you as an example.

A. chair [t͡ʃɛɹ]/ [t͡ʃeɹ]

B. roar _____

C. part _____

D. error _____

E. burn _____

F. ear _____

G. fair _____

H. urn _____

I. quart _____

---

1 Although a point made more clearly in Chapter Six of the textbook, symbols inside of slanted brackets represent the phoneme, an abstract mental categorization of a set of similar sounds. Those similar sounds occur in specific words and in specific phonetic environments. We are using /r/ here to capture the very general r-sound of English, but that /r/ might be realized in a number of ways depending on position in the word and the specific variety of English it is spoken in.

2-2. Working with a Tap

In some varieties of English, including Standard American English, alveolar stops, when pronounced between two vowels, will shorten, resulting in a short, voiced tap of the tongue tip in the alveolar region of the mouth. The phonetic symbol for that tap is [ɾ]. (This is the same sound as the "r simple" in Spanish, as in the word *pero*, meaning 'but.') However, the tap does not always occur between vowels. Consider the following list of words with /t/ or /d/ between vowels. (Note the double spelling of the consonant as <tt>[2] or <dd> has nothing to do with the phonetic realization of those consonants.) Indicate which words contain a tap by writing "tap" in the blank following the word.

A. attach _____

B. batter _____

C. ladder _____

D. letter _____

E. atomic _____

F. fanatic _____

G. adore _____

H. added _____

I. martyr _____

J. bedding _____

K. attic _____

L. ado _____

M. batty _____

N. atone _____

O. bedazzle _____

P. Otto _____

Q. motel _____

R. reduce _____

S. meaty _____

T. odious _____

Now considering the words in the list above, where does the stress fall on each word. Indicate that stress by marking the stressed syllable with an acute accent (´). What pattern did you find? When does tapping occur?

---

2 Recall from the textbook that spelling symbols are represented between angled brackets, < >.

2-3. Transcribing Words with a Tap

Transcribe the following words, taking care to note whether the medial consonant is [t], [d], or [ɾ]. The first is completed for you as an example.

A. battle   [bæɾəl][3]

B. attic   _____

C. atomic   _____

D. motel   _____

E. reduce   _____

F. letter   _____

G. latter   _____

H. atone   _____

I. meaty   _____

J. ado   _____

2-4. Working with Syllabic Consonants

Very often the weight of a syllable is carried by a vowel. For example, in a word like *communication* [kəmjunɪkeʃən], there are five vowels and five syllables, each vowel being the nucleus of the syllable. However, it is not only vowels that can act as the nucleus of the syllable, and in fact some consonants can carry syllabic weight. In English, these consonants are typically nasals and liquids. Consider a word like *bottle*. Unless you are being very careful in your speech, it is most likely that you do not have a vowel in the second syllable but instead shift the weight of the syllable onto the /l/. The symbol for syllabicity is a short vertical line under the consonant.[4] Consider these examples.

bottle [bɑɾl̩]
written [ɹɪʔn̩]
bottom [bɑɾm̩]

---

3   In the next exercise, you will deal with the final l-sound in words such as this one in more detail.

4   In an earlier exercise, you were introduced to /r/-colored schwa, [ɚ]. Practically speaking, there is no phonetic difference between [ɚ] and [ɹ̩]; the difference is perhaps better thought of as theoretical in nature. For this exercise, use [ɹ̩] in keeping with the other symbols in the exercise.

Transcribe the following words spoken in natural, casual speech, taking care to note syllabic consonants. The first is completed for you as an example.

A. writer   [ɹaɪɾɹ̩]

B. mitten   _____

C. battle   _____

D. litter   _____

E. cuddle   _____

F. button   _____

G. acre   _____

H. shovel   _____

I. Latin   _____

J. ever   _____

2-5. Minimal Pairs

Minimal pairs refer to two words that contrast in one sound at the same place in both words. Thus, *light~right*, *either~ether*, and *back~batch* are all minimal pairs showing the contrastive sounds in initial, medial, and final positions, respectively. One of the reasons that the contrast is important is that it tells us that the two contrasting sounds must be quite important in their mental status, and as we will see later, that distinctive status brings us to another area concerning the study of sounds: phonology.

In this exercise, describe the contrasting sounds in the following sets of minimal pairs. Be sure to state where the contrast is located in the two words. The first is completed for you as an example.

A. a. teeth   b. teethe
The two words contrast in final position, a. containing a voiceless interdental fricative and b. a voiced interdental fricative.

B. a. miss   b. kiss

_____

_____

C. a. rock   b. rack

_____

_____

D. a. love   b. shove

_____

_____

E. a. flan   b. flag

_____

_____

F. a. ill   b. ale

_____

_____

G. a. crack   b. crab

_____

_____

H. a. peel   b. deal

_____

_____

I. a. book   b. bush

_____

_____

J. a. brie   b. brew

_____

_____

K. a. jug   b. judge

_____

_____

2-6. Natural Classes

One of the many reasons that it is important to know phonetics for studying the history of a language is the fact that many sound changes affect not only individual sounds but groups of sounds that are similar in some way. In phonetics and phonology, such groups are referred to as "natural classes." In this exercise, consider the groups of sounds in each line and state the common articulatory features of each set. The first is completed for you as an example.

A. [k], [g], [ŋ]
   The three sounds all share the feature of having a velar articulation.

B. [p], [t], [k]

   _____

   _____

C. [m], [ŋ], [n]

   _____

   _____

D. [i], [u], [ɪ]

   _____

   _____

E. [b], [m], [dʒ]

   _____

   _____

F. [o], [e], [ɔ]

   _____

   _____

G. [s], [v], [ʃ]

   _____

   _____

H. [t], [s], [ɹ]

_____

_____

I. [k], [g], [ŋ]

_____

_____

J. [u], [ɔ], [ɑ]

_____

_____

K. [b], [dʒ], [j]

_____

_____

PART THREE: ADVANCED EXERCISES

3-1. Fast vs. Slow Speech

A difficulty that students encounter when learning phonetics is that they realize that they do not pronounce the same word in the same way in every situation. While the ideal of a standard pronunciation leads many to believe that there is one and only one (correct) way of saying a word, even the slightest attention to actual language use shows that speakers vary their speech in terms of pronunciation and grammar to fit the linguistic situation. For instance, we don't speak to our closest friends and family in the same way we greet a receptionist in a doctor's office. In formal or official situations, we tend to talk more slowly and to enunciate sounds more carefully. In casual situations, we speak faster and allow sounds to affect one another in ways that cause some sounds to be dropped or to become more like the sounds around them.

In this exercise, consider each pair of sentences. The first is a representation of slower, more careful speech and the second faster, more casual speech. What differences between the two do you observe? The first is completed for you as an example.

A. [maɹi kæn gɪv ju ðə ditelz]
   [maɹi kæŋ gɪv jə ðə ditelz]

   The alveolar [n] in the word "can" in the first sentence has changed to a velar [ŋ] and the vowel [u] in "you" in the first sentence has changed to a schwa, [ə].

B. [səlinə wɔɹkt bai ðə faiɹ]
   [səlinə wɪk bai ðə faiɹ]

   _____

   _____

C. [wi lɚnd ðæt ɪn ɛlɪmɛntəɹi skul]
   [wi lɪ̩n ðæt ɪn ɛlɪmɛntɹiskul]

   _____

   _____

D. [ai dont biliv wət ju sɔ]
   [ai dont biliv wətʃu sɔ]

   _____

   _____

E. [ðə pɛtstɔɹ sold hæmstɹz]
    [ðə pɛʔ stɔɹ sold hæmpstɹz]

_____

_____

3-2. Assimilation

In exercise 3-1, you saw this sentence pair:

[maɹri kæn gɪv ju ðə ditelz]
[maɹri kæŋ gɪv jə ðə ditelz]

One of the things that you may have noticed was that the [n] of [kæn] from the more formal representation of that sentence changed to a [ŋ] in casual speech. What you observed was a very common process in speech known as "assimilation." Assimilation refers to the phenomenon that sounds (often adjacent sounds, but sometimes sounds at a distance from one another) become more alike in some feature or another. In the example here, the alveolar [n] becomes velar [ŋ] in anticipation of the velar [g] in the following word *go*.

In this exercise, consider each of the strings of words and describe the assimilation pattern you see in phonetic terms. The first one is completed for you as an example.

A. [əɹendʒmɛnts hæv ɔlɹɛɾi bɪn med]
    [əɹendʒmɛnts hæv ɔlɹɛɾi bɪm med]

The alveolar [n] in the first sentence has changed into the bilabial [m] in assimilation with the following bilabial [m] in made.

B. [wʊd ju hɛlp mi]
    [wʊdʒu hɛlp mi]

_____

_____

C. [ɑi wɪl mɪs ju]
    [ɑi wɪl mɪʃju]

_____

_____

D. [ɪts ən ɔŋgoɪŋ prɑblɛm]
[ɪts ən ɔŋgoɪŋ prɑblɛm]

_____

_____

E. [ʃi sɛd ʃi nouz ju]
[ʃi sɛd ʃi nouʒju]

_____

_____

F. [ɑi kæn mit ju]
[ɑi kæm mitʃu]

_____

_____

3-3. Things We Don't Hear, until We Take Phonetics

As you have undoubtedly become aware during your study of phonetics, we simply do not hear many of the sounds of our own speech on a conscious level most of the time. In this exercise, your attention will be drawn to a few more very subtle features of speech as a way of expanding your knowledge of phonetics.

Say out loud the words in list A and then the words in list B. As you say them, hold your hand in front of your mouth and pay attention to your breath.

<u>A</u>	<u>B</u>
take	stake
tear (as in "rip")	stare
top	stop
toll	stole
talk	stalk
tint	stint
tale	stale
tack	stack
tough	stuff

You probably noticed that the "t" sound in the words in list A was accompanied by a puff of air, whereas the "t"s in list B were not. The puff that you experienced is called "aspiration," which is indicated in phonetics with a raised "h": [tʰ]. The unaspirated "t"s are just [t].

Now, as it happens, the occurrence of aspiration is not random. What is the pattern? That is, where do [tʰ] and [t] occur in the lists of words in columns A and B?

_____

_____

Can you discern a similar pattern in the following lists?

A	B	C	D
pot	spot	key	ski
pear	spare	cold	scold
peak	speak	kill	skill
pit	spit	crawl	scrawl
pool	spool	core	score
park	spark	Kate	skate
pun	spun	can	scan
pie	spy	cape	scape

Can you state the pattern now more generally using the notion of a natural class (see again exercise 2-6)?

_____

_____

Now consider the "k" and "p" sounds in the following sets of words.

Asprirated	Unaspirated
decapitate	decal
oppose	opposite
mechanic	Michael
repeat	repetition
occur	reckon
deposit	deposition
décor	decoration

What seems to be controlling aspiration in these sets of words? (Hint: determine where the stress falls in each one.)

_____

_____

How is this similar to the pattern you saw in exercise 2-2 in this chapter?

_____

_____

Notes

_____

_____

_____

_____

_____

_____

_____

_____

_____

_____

_____

_____

_____

_____

_____

_____

_____

_____

_____

_____

_____

_____

_____

_____

_____

_____

_____

_____

_____

Notes

Chapter Five

1-1. Germanic Languages

Fill in the blanks in the following branch for Germanic languages of the Indo-European family, indicating where the following languages should be placed: German, Swedish, Gothic, Icelandic, Yiddish, English, Norwegian, Dutch, Faroese, Frisian.

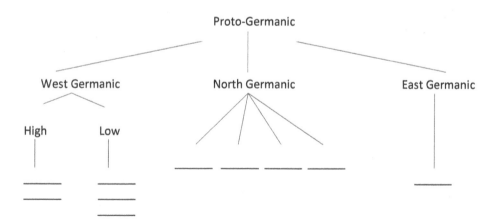

1-2. Indo-European Homeland

On the map provided, shade in the area where speakers of Indo-European are believed to have originated.

1-3. Grimm's Law

Complete the sound correspondences between Indo-European and Germanic according to Grimm's Law as described in the textbook.

	Indo-European		Germanic
A.	Voiceless Stops	>	Voiceless Fricatives
	p	>	—
	—	>	θ
	k	>	—
B.	Voiced Stops	>	Voiceless Stops
	—	>	p
	—	>	t
	g	>	—
C.	Aspirated Voiced Stops	>	Unaspirated Voiced Stops
	bh	>	—
	—	>	d
	gh	>	—

1-4. Strong and Weak Verbs

Consider the simple present and simple past forms in the following Germanic languages. Which form is a weak verb and which is a strong verb based on what you know from the description of strong and weak verbs in the textbook? The first is completed for you as an example.

German

Infinitive	Past Tense	Strong or Weak
A. lieben 'to love'	liebte 'loved'	*weak*
B. befehlen 'to command'	befahl 'commanded'	_____
C. mahlen 'to paint'	mahlte 'painted'	_____
D. salzen 'to salt'	salzte 'salted'	_____
E. helfen 'to help'	half 'helped'	_____

Swedish

Infinitive	Past Tense	Strong or Weak
F. betala 'to pay'	betalade 'paid'	_____
G. brinna 'to burn'	brann 'burned'	_____
H. dricka 'to drink'	drack 'drank'	_____
I. skilja 'to separate'	skiljde 'separated'	_____

Icelandic

Infinitive	Past Tense	Strong or Weak
J. aga 'to discipline'	agaði 'disciplined'	_____
K. afsaka 'to pardon'	afsakaði 'pardoned'	_____
L. drepa 'to beat'	drap 'beat'	_____
M. fljúga 'to fly'	flaug 'flew'	_____
N. kála 'to kill'	kálaði 'killed'	_____

Gothic

Infinitive	Past Tense	Strong or Weak
O. rinna 'to run'	rann 'ran'	_____
P. nasjan 'to save'	nasida 'saved'	_____
Q. niman 'to take'	nam 'took'	_____
R. salbōn 'to anoint'	salbōda 'anointed'	_____

Dutch

Infinitive	Past Tense	Strong or Weak
S. hoop 'to hope'	hoopte 'hoped'	_____
T. schaven 'to hew'	schaafde[1] 'hewed'	_____
U. geven 'to give'	gaf 'gave'	_____
V. kijken 'to look'	keek 'looked'	_____
W. komen 'to come'	kwam 'came'	_____

---

1 Note that the doubled <a> is merely orthographic in Dutch and does not change the quality of the vowel in the verb.

PART TWO: INTERMEDIATE EXERCISES

2-1. Features of Germanic Languages

List the five features of Germanic languages presented in the textbook and exemplify each. While you can certainly find examples in the book, try to find new examples for at least some of the features.

Feature   Example

A. _____   _____

B. _____   _____

C. _____   _____

D. _____   _____

E. _____   _____

2-2. Examine the following passages. One is from a linguistics textbook and the other is a transcript of natural, conversational speech. List all of the verb forms, both synthetic and periphrastic, from each and then consider the questions that follow.

Text One (from Frederick J. Newmeyer, *Grammatical Theory: Its Limits and Its Possibilities*, Chicago: Chicago University Press, 1983. This is the first paragraph of the Preface.)

This book is for anyone who feels frustrated after his or her first exposure to generative grammar. Even many people who have succeeded in mastering the difficult formalism and unfamiliar style of argumentation are apt to leave their introductory course with the feeling that they have learned little more than a novel way of "playing with symbols" (to use an often-heard expression) and have achieved little insight into how language "really works." My goal here is to put forward the best case I can that any explanatory account of the workings of language must include, as a central component, a formal grammar. I have a two-part strategy for achieving this goal. The first is to document the ways the basic notions of generativist theory receive independent support from research outside the domain of grammar proper. The second is to show that generativist theory, in turn, has helped contribute to the explanations of a number of phenomena that most people would not regard as strictly grammatical.

Text Two (adapted from a dialogue from Gillian Brown and George Yule, *Discourse Analysis*, Cambridge: Cambridge University Press, 1983:85. The speakers are from

Edinburgh, Scotland, and some grammatical forms and dysfluencies have been regularized for familiarity to a larger English-speaking audience.)

Man 1: Oh I did odd jobs like paper boy and chemist's shop... worked in a chemist's shop and did two or three others and I finally started in the bricklaying so I served my time as a bricklayer.

Man 2: That's good money.

Man 1: Nowadays it is but in that time it wasn't. It was only three pounds nine a week so...

Man 2: My father was a stonemason and he started at home and they were paid a halfpenny an hour extra for being left-handed.

A. What is the most frequent verb form for each text?
B. What is the second most frequent?
C. What is the ratio of synthetic forms to periphrastic forms in each?
D. What do you think accounts for the different frequencies of verb forms between the two genre types?

PART THREE: ADVANCED EXERCISES

3-1. Strong and Weak Adjectives

Based on what you know about strong and weak adjectives in old and modern Germanic languages, determine whether the italicized adjective in the following sentences is weak or strong. You may want to review the distribution of weak and strong adjectives from Chapter Five in the textbook. The first is completed for you as an example.

A. Dutch  Strong or Weak

Marten had een *groot* huis, maar het was te   groot en hij heft het verkoopt.
Marten had a   big   house. But it was too   big   and he has it sold
'Marten had a big house but it was too big and he sold it.'

B. German   Strong or Weak

Die zwei *junge* Mädchen sind nach Frankreich gefahren
The two young girls   are to   France   traveled
'The two young girls traveled to France.'

C. Gothic   Strong or Weak

Sa *blinda* manna habaida gast
The blind   man   had   guest
'The blind man had a guest.'

D. Icelandic   Strong or Weak

Rauður hestur var tekinn til dýralæknisins
Red   horse was taken to vet
'A red horse was taken to the vet.'

E. Swedish   Strong or Weak

Den *gamla* stolen kastades   bort
The old   chair was thrown away
'The old chair was thrown away.'

F. Old English   Strong or Weak

Ic hæbbe *strangne* mann gesawen
I have   strong   man seen
'I have seen a strong man.'

3-2. New Verbal Periphrases in English

Even though Germanic languages have, strictly speaking, a two-tense system, that identity only takes into consideration synthetic verb forms, that is, the simple present and the simple past. However, all modern, and even older, Germanic languages carry out some of their temporal and aspectual work though verbal periphrasis. The development of new verbal periphrases in Germanic languages, including English, continues even today. In this exercise, consider the verbal periphrasis in English italicized in each of the sentences below and attempt to describe what the periphrasis means. Note that some of the examples will be non-Standard English or from varieties of English you might not know, and so you may have to research their meanings or ask your classmates for their input.

A. I don't think the government *is gonna fund* Dr. Hairbrain's research much longer.

B. Our neighbors *were fixin' to move* but I think they decided to stay.

C. I *ain't tryna fail* this class, but the work is hard!

D. The townsfolk *were just after comin'* home from church when they learned the terrible news.

E. There *ain't finna be* many more chances like this one.

F. Our brothers *were a-workin'* hard down the mines in those days.

G. You *done messed up*, son! Messed up, real bad.

Notes

Notes

_____

_____

_____

_____

_____

_____

_____

_____

_____

_____

_____

_____

_____

_____

_____

_____

_____

_____

_____

_____

_____

_____

_____

_____

_____

_____

_____

Chapter Six

You probably noticed that Chapter Six is the shortest chapter of the textbook and it covers just a few concepts. However, those concepts are central to historical work in a language. The workbook, therefore, will expand your knowledge of those concepts through additional explanation and exercises on those concepts.

1-1. Classical Phoneme Theory

In the textbook, you read that phonemes were abstract mental categories of sounds and that allophones were the actual speech manifestations of those sounds. In fact, you have already had some experience working with phonemes and allophones from Chapter Four of this workbook in which you discerned a pattern involving aspiration of voiceless stops. The solution to that pattern was that the voiceless stops were aspirated at the beginning of a word or before a stressed syllable within a word. Thus the k-sounds in *catch* and *occult* are both realized with aspiration, [kʰ], while the k-sound after [s], as in *scout*, is not; it is simply [k].

Applying our definitions of phoneme and allophone, we recognize that what we are calling here a "k-sound" refers to the phoneme /k/ (phonemes are written between slanted lines) while [kʰ] and [k] are allophones of the phoneme /k/ (actual speech sounds are written in square brackets). In other words, the idea of the k-sound, that is the phoneme /k/, is the category that we store in our minds as part of our knowledge of English. [kʰ] and [k] are the actual ways that /k/ can sound in speech.

Now, concentrate on the distribution of [kʰ] and [k]. We have said that the first happens at the beginning of a word or before a stressed syllable in the word, and that the second occurs after [s]. We expect this distribution to be true all of the time.

A. Think of five one-syllable words that have /k/ at the beginning of the word or at the beginning of a stressed syllable within a word. Then, think of five words in which /k/ follows [s]. The first is completed for you as an example.

/k/ beginning of word   /k/ after [s]
or before stressed syllable

catch   *skeet*

_____   _____

_____   _____

_____   _____

Does that pattern hold true for each of the words?

B. Now invent five completely made-up one-syllable words that could happen in English with a /k/ at the beginning of the word or at the beginning of a stressed syllable within a word. Next, invent five completely made-up words that could happen in English with a /k/ after [s]. The first is completed for you as an example.

/k/ beginning of word   /k/ after [s]
or before stressed syllable

kafe   *skush*

_____   _____

_____   _____

_____   _____

Does the pattern still hold?

1-2. Complementary Distribution

What you should have found in exercise 1-1 is that [kʰ] always occurred at the beginning of a word or before a stressed syllable and that [k] always occurred after [s]—even when you made the words up! In other words, [kʰ] and [k] never occurred in the same place; you didn't randomly get [kʰ] after [s], for instance. This property of allophones is called complementary distribution: where one sound occurs, the other doesn't. (As a non-linguistic example, you can think about Clark Kent and Superman; they are in complementary distribution since whenever one appears, the other cannot.)

A. In this exercise, consider the letters X and Y among the sequences of letters in the first column and second column. Are the two letters in complementary distribution in the first and second columns? How did you determine your answer? (For this exercise, X or Y at the beginning of the sequence is said to be preceded by nothing (= ø), and X at the end of a sequence is said to be followed by nothing (=ø).)

First Column	Second Column
GJLXN	UUUYK
XUIKM	PJYNT
OXBPU	YYYYY
NTWEX	BOPYN
QXBCO	HYIYE

B. Are X and Y in complementary distribution between the two columns here? How did you determine your answer?

First Column	Second Column
NXTBD	OIYVG
MIXVE	UJNY
XOPRT	YOLIM
UIGXE	RTYER
WSCPX	IANYT

1-3. Contrastive Sounds

Another central concept of classical phoneme theory is that of contrast. Phonemes are said to be contrastive because they have the ability to create different words. Analyze the words in the following list. Are [g] and [kʰ]/[k] in complementary distribution? (We already determined above that [k]/[kʰ] were allophones of a single phoneme so we do not expect them to occur in the same position of a word. Our interest here is comparing [g] to [kʰ] and [k], as a group.)

wick	degree	gap
Eggo	smock	decree
smog	echo	wig
cap	gash	cash

We are safe to say that [g], on the one hand, and [kʰ]/[k], on the other, represent different phonemes since they are not in complementary distribution, and we notice that there are many instances in which either [g] or [kʰ]/[k] can occur in the same position of a word. But crucially, when they do occur in the same position of a word, they create different meanings; *cap* and *gap* are different words.

In classical phoneme theory, words like *cap* and *gap* are said to be a minimal pair, two words that differ by only one sound at the same place in the word with the result of having two different meanings. Other minimal pairs from English would include *tea* and *key* (which differ in [tʰ] and [kʰ] at the beginning of the word), *up* and *of* (which differ in [p] and [v] at the end of the word), and *muffle* and *muddle* (which differ in [f] and [ɾ] in the middle of the word). Thus we conclude that [tʰ] and [kʰ] are from different phonemes, /t/ and /k/. Similarly, [p] and [v] are from /p/ and /v/ and [f] and [ɾ] are from /f/ and /d/ (on the distribution of tap [ɾ], see again exercise 2-3 in Chapter Four of the workbook).

Place each of the minimal pairs in the following list side by side and determine the sound that contrasts the two words. Based on your list, how many different phonemes can you distinguish? The first is completed for you as an example.

rife	pale	four	shove
soup	song	zip	poor
fat	long	shale	sip
fab	coup	shut	
hair	ripe	bear	

A. Minimal Pair *rife and ripe*.   Contrasting sounds */f/ and /p/*.

B. Minimal Pair _____and _____.   Contrasting sounds _____ and _____.

C. Minimal Pair _____and _____.   Contrasting sounds _____ and _____.

D. Minimal Pair _____and _____.   Contrasting sounds _____ and _____.

E. Minimal Pair _____and _____.   Contrasting sounds _____ and _____.

F. Minimal Pair _____and _____.   Contrasting sounds _____ and _____.

G. Minimal Pair _____and _____.   Contrasting sounds _____ and _____.

H. Minimal Pair _____and _____.   Contrasting sounds _____ and _____.

I. Minimal Pair _____and _____.   Contrasting sounds _____ and _____.

1-4. Minimal Pairs in English

In exercise 1-3 above, the contrastive sound of each minimal pair was either at the beginning or the end of the word and all involved consonants, but in fact minimal pairs may occur in other positions of the word and involve vowel sounds as well. From the following list, pick out all of the minimal pairs and state which sounds contrast and what their positions in the words are. Note that the contrasting sounds may appear in any position in the word and may involve vowels as well as consonants. The first is completed for you as an example.

leisure	cluck	book	leak
tear	reek	leader	amiss
sing	rack	song	thigh
alone	club	fair	go
took	art	thy	atone
low	lack	abyss	
arm	braid	brood	

A. Minimal Pair: *leisure and leader* Contrasting sounds: */ʒ/ and /d/*
   Contrast location: *second consonant of the words*

B. Minimal Pair _____and _____. Contrasting sounds _____ and _____.
   Contrast location: _____

C. Minimal Pair _____and _____. Contrasting sounds _____ and _____.
   Contrast location: _____

D. Minimal Pair _____and _____. Contrasting sounds _____ and _____.
   Contrast location: _____

E. Minimal Pair _____and _____. Contrasting sounds _____ and _____.
   Contrast location: _____

F. Minimal Pair _____and _____. Contrasting sounds _____ and _____.
   Contrast location: _____

G. Minimal Pair _____and _____. Contrasting sounds _____ and _____.
   Contrast location: _____

H. Minimal Pair _____and _____. Contrasting sounds _____ and _____.
   Contrast location: _____

I. Minimal Pair _____and _____. Contrasting sounds _____ and _____.
   Contrast location: _____

J. Minimal Pair _____and _____. Contrasting sounds _____ and _____.
   Contrast location: _____

K. Minimal Pair _____and _____. Contrasting sounds _____ and _____.
Contrast location: _____

L. Minimal Pair _____and _____. Contrasting sounds _____ and _____.
Contrast location: _____

M. Minimal Pair _____and _____. Contrasting sounds _____ and _____.
Contrast location: _____

1-5. Phonology: English /n/

The English sound /n/ can have several allophonic realizations: [ɱ] voiced, labio-dental, nasal (like pronouncing a [f] or [v] through your nose); [n̪] voiced, interdental, nasal (like pronouncing a "th" through your nose); [ŋ] voiced, velar, nasal; and, of course, [n] voiced, alveolar nasal. Consider the following list and determine the pattern for when [ɱ], [n̪], [ŋ], and [n] occur among these words. The pronunciation of each word is given. (The pronunciation here represents the variety of American English spoken by one of the authors.)

infamous	[ɪɱfəməs]
enthusiastic	[ɛn̪θuziæstɪk]
anthropology	[æn̪θɹopalədʒi]
ingrained	[ɪŋgɹend]
invitation	[ɪɱvɪteʃən]
angry	[eŋgɹi]
enthralling	[ɛn̪θɹɔlɪŋ]
incognito	[ɪŋkagniɾo]
ungrateful	[əŋgɹetfəl]
invariable	[ɪɱvɛɹiəbəl]
in there	[ɪn̪ðɛɹ]
infamy	[ɪɱfəmi]
ankle	[eŋkəl]
infernal	[ɪɱfɚnəl]
enthrone	[ɛn̪θɹon]
incomplete	[ɪŋkɔmplit]
invective	[ɪɱvektɪv]
unthinkable	[ən̪θɪŋkəbəl]

A. Where does [ɱ] occur?   _____

B. Where does [ɳ] occur?   _____

C. Where does [ŋ] occur?   _____

D. Where does [n] occur?   _____

1-6. Spanish Phonology

Consider the following words from Spanish. What is the status of [s] and [z]? Do they represent sounds from different phonemes or are they allophones of the same phoneme? If you determine that they are in allophonic distribution, state the conditioning environment for each. (The Spanish represented here is Standard Costa Rican pronunciation. [β] is a voiced bilabial fricative, and [ɣ] is a voiced velar fricative. The rest of the symbols should be familiar to you from the phonetics you learned in Chapter Four.)

desde	[dɛzde]	'since'
busco	[busko]	'I search'
esbeltez	[ezβɛltes]	'thinness'
esbozar	[ezβosɑr]	'to sketch'
esposo	[espɔso]	'husband'
esgrimir	[ezɣrimir]	'to handle a sword'
soba	[soβɑ]	'kneading'
salud	[sɑluð]	'health'
vacas	[bɑcɑs]	'cows'
libros	[liβros]	'books'
desnudo	[dɛznuðo]	'naked'
disparo	[dispɑro]	'shot (of a gun)'
dislate	[dizlɑte]	'silly thing'
desverar	[dezβerɑr]	'to refloat'
despedir	[despeðir]	'to say good bye'
obstar	[obstɑr]	'to hinder'
oscilar	[oskilɑr]	'to swing'
pasar	[pɑsɑr]	'to pass'
pasmado	[pɑzmɑðo]	'amazed'
deseo	[deseo]	'a wish'

_____

_____

1-7. Inflectional vs. Derivational Morphology

The textbook introduced you to inflectional and derivational morphology, and this exercise is designed to expand your knowledge of that difference.

Derivational morphology:
1. creates a new word;
2. sometimes changes the part of speech of the word to which it is added;
3. is sensitive to the group of words it may attach to—that is, if a given derivational morpheme attaches to verbs to make nouns, it won't attach to all verbs.

Inflectional morphology:
1. does not create a new word but merely a different form of the same word;
2. never changes the part of speech of the word it is attached to;
3. attaches to all relevant members of a class—that is, if the inflectional affix attaches to lexical verbs, it should attach to all lexical verbs (although, as we will see, this is not always the case).

Applying the three criteria just given for derivational and inflectional morphology, identify which of the suffixes in the following sets is derivational and which is inflectional. (You may need to refer back to Chapter Two in the textbook if you don't recognize some of the terminology here.) The first is completed for you as an example.

A. -s (third person singular present tense, as in *he drives*) versus *-ity* (as in *purity*)

In the above pair, -s is an inflectional morpheme because:

1. *It did not create a new word, but a different form of the same word. Drives in he drives is the same word as drive in they drive.*
2. *It did not change the part of speech: drive is a verb, drives is a form of that verb.*
3. *It will attach to all lexical verbs: he drives, he talks, he dances, he writes, he jumps, etc.*

   -ity is a derivational morpheme because:

1. *It created a new word; pure is not the same word as purity.*
2. *It changed the part of speech from an adjective pure to a noun purity.*
3. *It does not attach to all adjectives to make nouns. It works for pure--> purity, secure--> security, serene--> serenity, etc. but not big--> biggity or green--> greenity, etc.*

B. *-dom* (as in *kingdom*) versus *-ing* (as in *running* in a sentence like "He is running.")

_____

_____

_____

_____

_____

_____

_____

_____

C. *-ed* (regular past tense, as in *like* --> *liked*) versus *-al* (as in *architecture* --> *architectural*)

_____

_____

_____

_____

_____

_____

_____

D. *-s* (regular plural, as in *book* --> *books*) versus *-ic* (as in *myth* --> *mythic*)

_____

_____

_____

_____

_____

_____

_____

PART TWO: INTERMEDIATE EXERCISES

2-1. Minimal Pairs

In 1-3 and 1-4 you worked with the concept of the minimal pairs test. In this exercise, create minimal pairs for the description given. The first is completed for you as an example.

A. [b]-[f] word initially *ban* and *fan*

B. [dʒ]-[k] word finally _____ and _____

C. [ʃ]-[l] word medially _____ and _____

D. [tʃ]-[ɹ] word medially _____ and _____

E. [t]-[b] word finally _____ and _____

F. [æ]-[e] word initially _____ and _____

G. [ʌ]-[u] word medially _____ and _____

H. [m]-[ŋ] word finally _____ and _____

I. [i]-[o] word finally _____ and _____

J. [w]-[g] word initially _____ and _____

2-2. Sonorant Devoicing

The nasals /m/ and /n/ and are normally voiced, but under certain circumstances they may be devoiced and occur as [m̥, n̥].[1] The same is true for liquids /l, r/ and glides /w, j/, which may all occur as voiceless [l̥, ɹ̥, w̥, j̥]. Nasals and liquids (and sometimes glides) together are called "sonorants." Consider the words below and determine the phonetic environment that devoices sonorants and glides in English.

plaid	[pl̥æd]
blame	[blem]
cradle	[kɹ̥erəl]
kraken	[kɹ̥ækən]
drive	[dɹɑɪv]
green	[gɹin]
queen	[kw̥in]
Gwen	[gwɛn]
twin	[tw̥ɪn]
cute	[kj̥ut]
beauty	[bjuti]
cube	[kj̥ub]

---

1 Theoretically the devoicing could also happen with /ŋ/, but /ŋ/ because of its limited distribution does not occur in positions where such devoicing could affect it. Note that a small subscript circle indicates voicelessness on a symbol that would otherwise represent a voiced sound.

What is the environment that causes devoicing of sonorants in English?

_____

_____

2-3. Japanese Phonology

This exercise presents you with a list of Japanese words. For each word you have the phonemic spelling of the word and after that the phonetic spelling. Focus on the phoneme /t/.

/anata/	[anata]	'you'
/koti/	[kotʃi]	'there'
/tako/	[tako]	'octopus'
/tenki/	[teŋki]	'weather'
/moti/	[motʃi]	'possess'
/iti/	[itʃi]	'one'
/tati/	[tatʃi]	'we'
/tiba/	[tʃiba]	'the name of a Japanese prefecture'
/tiko/	[tʃiko]	'a girl's name'
/kata/	[kata]	'people'
/bito/	[bito]	'by'

What are the possible allophonic variants of /t/ and where do they occur?

_____

_____

2-4. Oriya Morphology

Consider the following morphological processes in Oriya (an Indo-European language of the Indic branch, spoken in northern India). First, state in general terms what morpheme has been added, being sure to identify it as a prefix or a suffix. Next, describe the meaning change it has made. Finally, applying the three criteria for derivational versus inflectional morphology laid out in 1-7, determine whether the process is inflectional or derivational. Express your reasoning explicitly. (Sometimes more than one example is given to help you see the pattern more clearly.) The first is completed for you as an example.

A. krɔyɔ   buying   bi-krɔyɔ   selling

A prefix, *bi-*, has been added to the word. The prefix appears to be derivational since it has the effect of creating a new word.

B. kha   eat   kha-e   I eat
    pɔdh   read   pɔdh-e   I read
    hɔs   laugh   hɔs-e   I laugh

_____

_____

C. soṅgo   friend   ni-soṅgo   friendless

_____

_____

D. ramɔ   Rama (name) ramɔku   Rama, accusative
                                         form (as object)

    sapɔ   snake   sapɔku   snake, accusative
                                         form

    musa   mouse   musaku   mouse, accusative
                                         form

_____

_____

E. pagɔla   insane   pagɔḷakhana mental asylum
    ḍaktɔr   doctor   ḍaktɔrkhana hospital
    khɔjoṇa   tax money   khɔjonakhaṇa treasury

_____

_____

F. debɔta   god   debɔtamane   gods
    pokɔ   bug   pokɔmane   bugs
    pila   child   pilamane   children

_____

_____

G. boka   fool   bokami   foolishness
    pila   childish   pilami   childishness

_____

_____

H. rɔktɔ   blood   rɔktaktɔ   bloody
    bisɔ   poison   bisaktɔ   poisonous

_____

_____

I. kha   eat   khaib   will eat
    pɔdh   read   pɔdhib   will read
    bɔs   laugh   bɔsib   will laugh

_____

_____

PART THREE: ADVANCED EXERCISES

3-1. Allophones?

In exercise 1-1, you learned that allophones are in complementary distribution and in exercises 1-2, 2-1, and 2-2, you relied on complementary distribution to determine whether two sounds bore a phonemic or allophonic relationship to one another. However, is it possible for two sounds to be in complementary distribution yet not be allophones of the same phoneme? Consider the words in the following list from English.

hand	hopeful	linger
anger	who	happy
hover	rang	anchor
sing	mingle	hike
bank	gong	blinker

A. What is the distribution of [ŋ] and [h]?

_____

B. Do you believe it is reasonable to consider [ŋ] and [h] as allophones of the same phoneme even though they are in complementary distribution in English? Why or why not?

_____

_____

_____

3-2. Minimal Pairs in Yoeme

In exercise 1-4, you selected words from English that made up minimal pairs. In this exercise, you will do the same thing for a language that you are likely unfamiliar with, Yoeme. Yoeme is a Native American language spoken by the Yaqui tribe in the American Southwest and northern Mexico. For this exercise, you may consider the spellings to be fairly straightforward phonetic spellings. Note there are only seven minimal pairs, so many words listed are only there as distractors! (Note that <ch> should be considered a single sound, [tʃ].) The first is completed for you as an example.

ata	'we'
puhta	'blow away'
veha	'already'

kova	'head'
haita	'despise'
vamsi	'be in a hurry'
chaya	'tether it'
nat	'on each other'
yeeka	'able'
omta	'hate'
ota	'bone'
vai	'swell'
pua	'pick'
haal	'passage'
naup	'be hoarse'
vepa	'on top of'
maya	'toss at'
haaka	'grandmother'
komona	'get wet'
omna	'friend'
haiti	'messy'
yeecha	'put'
kotte	'break'
naaka	'daughter'

A. Minimal Pair *ata and ota*.   Contrasting sounds /a/ and /o/.

B. Minimal Pair _____ and _____. Contrasting sounds _____ and _____.

C. Minimal Pair _____ and _____. Contrasting sounds _____ and _____.

D. Minimal Pair _____ and _____. Contrasting sounds _____ and _____.

E. Minimal Pair _____ and _____. Contrasting sounds _____ and _____.

F. Minimal Pair _____ and _____. Contrasting sounds _____ and _____.

G. Minimal Pair _____ and _____. Contrasting sounds _____ and _____.

3-3. Sonorant Devoicing

In exercise 2-2, you determined the environment in which sonorants and glides lost at least some of their voicing. The relevant environment for that pattern in that exercise was always in a cluster after a voiceless consonant at the beginning of a word. What about that same environment in the middle of the word? Compare the columns of words below and answer the questions that follow.

A	B
accrue	acreage
besmear	plasma
between	fatwa
accumulate	accuracy
acclaim	recluse

A. Is the devoicing of the sonorant or glide more prominent in one or the other?

_____

B. What conditions the stronger devoicing?

_____

3-4. Vowel Reduction in English
Observe the vowel in the following sets of related word forms and first identify the vowel sound in each in the space provided. Then answer the questions that follow. (For this exercise, imagine the pronunciation as being quite casual; that is, don't over-pronounce the words.)

1	2	Vowel in 1	Vowel in 2
A. atom	atomic	_____	_____
B. maniac	maniacal	_____	_____
C. exclaim	exclamation	_____	_____
D. formulaic	formula	_____	_____
E. incremental	increment	_____	_____
F. solid	solidify	_____	_____
G. terrify	terrific	_____	_____
H. catastrophe	catastrophic	_____	_____
I. melody	melodic	_____	_____
J. comedy	comedian	_____	_____

What do the vowels in list 2 have in common?

_____

What seems to affect this particular kind of variation?

_____

3-5. Comparative Phonology: Dutch, English, and German

As you will likely know by now from the textbook, English, Dutch, and German are closely related languages. However, the phonology of Dutch differs from that of English and German in some ways. Consider the following words from the three languages and state that difference in phonetic terms. Note that the bolded syllable indicates that it is stressed. (Hint: you worked on this particular phonological pattern for English in exercise 1-1 in this chapter. Your answer should be an expansion of that to include the facts of German and Dutch.)

English	Dutch	German
peak [pʰik]	**pak** [pɑk] 'package'	**Pacht** [pʰaxt] 'lease'
ap**pear** [əpʰiɹ]	be**perk**t [bɛpɛrkt²] 'certain'	ent**pup**pen [ɛnpʰupɛn] 'emerge from cocoon'
take [tʰek]	**tegel** [tɛxɛl] 'tile'	**Tisch** [tʰɪʃ] 'table'
at**tire** [ətʰaɪɹ]	be**talen** [bɛtɑlən³] 'pay'	**Miss**ton [mɪstʰon] 'dissonance'
cook [kʰʊk]	**kap**per [kɑpɛr] 'hair dresser'	**Kohl** [kʰol] 'cabbage'
ar**cane** [ɑɹkʰen]	vo**kalen** [vokɑlən] 'vowels'	er**ken**nen [ɛkʰɛnɛn] 'to recognize'

_____

_____

_____

_____

3-6. Derivational and Inflectional Morphology

In some of the above exercises, you have based your determination that a morpheme is inflectional, at least in part, on the fact that the morpheme applied to many members of a class. In this exercise, you are asked to think about "exceptions" to certain inflectional patterns in English and to consider why they are "exceptional." (Note you may have to do some research in later parts of the textbook, or in other sources online or at a library.)

A. The plural suffix -s (sometimes written -es) attaches to nouns to show that more than one is being presented: one hat ~ two, three, 400 hats. Does every noun in English make its plural with -s? Make a list of nouns that are apparent "exceptions" and investigate the reasons that those nouns appear to be "exceptional."

_____

_____

---

2   There is a lot of variation in the pronunciation of Dutch /r/. For this exercise we will simply use the symbol [r].

3   The final [n] in this word and *vokalen* below are usually not pronounced in casual Dutch.

B. The third person singular present suffix -*s* attaches to verbs in agreement with a singular 3rd person subject: *he runs, Maria climbs, the giraffe eats,* etc. Does this -*s* attach to all verbs? What about a verb like *can*? Are there other verbs that behave like *can*? Why do you think such apparent "exceptions" occur among certain verbs?

_____

_____

3-7. Native and Borrowed Derivational Suffixes

Consider the following sets of derivational endings in English. Those in the first list are native suffixes, meaning that they date to the earliest forms of English and in some cases have clear cognates in other Germanic languages. The derivational suffixes in the second list are non-native suffixes, meaning that they have been borrowed into English during its history, either directly from Latin or from Latin through French.

Native Derivational Suffixes	Latin-/French-Borrowed Derivational Suffixes
-dom	-al
-ful	-ian
-hood	-ic
-ish	-ive
-less	-ity
-ness	-tion

Think of five words that have each of the endings above and consider the following questions:

A. Do both sets equally involve changes in the stem?[4]

_____

_____

---

4 "Stem" is the form of the word before any derivational or inflectional material is added to it. The "stem" of *loving* is *love* and that of *opacity* is *opaque*. Notice, however, that in the case of *love*, adding -*ing* did not alter the phonology of the stem. When -*ity* is added to the stem *opaque*, the final [k] sound is changed to [s]. In other words, the stem in *opacity* changed phonological shape.

B. Do both sets equally involve free bases? (When you remove the derivation, is the remaining part an independent word?)

_____

_____

Notes

Notes

_____

_____

_____

_____

_____

_____

_____

_____

_____

_____

_____

_____

_____

_____

_____

_____

_____

_____

_____

_____

_____

_____

_____

_____

_____

Chapter Seven

1-1. Orthography and Phonology: Single Words

Write the following OE words in PDE. The first is completed for you as an example.

A. pæð   *path*

B. Englisc   _____

C. scilling   _____

D. hecg   _____

E. diċ   _____

F. þorn   _____

G. dæġ   _____

H. sāriġ   _____

I. fæst   _____

J. wiċċecræft   _____

K. ðicnes   _____

L. ðancful   _____

1-2. Orthography and Phonology: Sentences

Write the following OE sentences in PDE. The first is completed for you as an example.

A. Ðæt is his scip.

That is his ship.

B. Fisc wæs in wætere.

_____

C. Ðæt ċild is yfel.

_____

D. Spellbōc wæs hefiġ.

_____

E. Smið dranc meolc.

_____

F. Hē wæs cræftiġ.

_____

1-3. Thinking about Case

This exercise is very similar to exercise 1-7 in Chapter Three of this workbook. Imagine that you understood what was the subject and the direct object of a sentence not by word order (the subject is before the verb, the direct object is after the verb) but by a marker at the end of the word.

In this exercise,
the marker for the subject will be * at the end of the noun phrase
the marker for the direct object will be % at the end of the noun phrase
the marker for the indirect object will be @ at the end of the noun phrase

Using the markers for subject, direct object, and indirect object, assemble the following strings of noun phrases and verbs into the regular order for Present-day English sentences. The first is completed for you as an example.

A. <u>Famous chefs%</u> had <u>fine ladies*</u>

Fine ladies had famous chefs.

B. <u>Famous chefs*</u> <u>crooked assistants%</u> hired.

_____

C. <u>Fine ladies%</u> <u>crooked assistants*</u> adored.

_____

D. <u>Crooked assistants* fine ladies%</u> adored.

_____

E. <u>Famous chefs* nervous lapdogs%</u> gave <u>fine ladies@</u>.

_____

F. <u>Nervous lapdogs% fine ladies*</u> gave <u>crooked assistants@</u>.

_____

1-4. Case in Old English

Languages like Old English, which have case systems, as in the sentences in the exercise above, employ markers on the nouns, adjectives, and determiners that indicate the function of the noun phrase in the sentence.

While the system in OE is much more complex than this, in the following exercise, we have selected one kind of noun and determiner in which you can determine if the noun phrase is the subject or the object by the form of the determiner.

When the noun is the subject, the determiner will be _se._
When the noun is the direct object, the determiner will be _þone._

Translate the following simple sentences. Remember that you will recognize what is the subject and what is the direct object not by word order but by the form of the determiner. The first is completed for you as an example.

A. <u>Se mann þone hund</u> lufode
   The man   the   dog   loved
   The man loved the dog.

B. <u>Se hlaford þone cyning</u> lufode
   The lord   the   king   loved

   _____

C. <u>þone scipmann se cyning</u> lufode
   the   shipman   the king   loved

   _____

D. <u>þone hund</u> <u>se scipman</u> lufode
   the   dog   the shipman   loved

_____

E. Lufode <u>se hund</u> <u>þone hlaford</u>
   Loved   the dog   the   lord

_____

1-5. The Verb

The verb in OE carries considerably more inflection than the verb in PDE. In the present tense, you can easily distinguish whether the subject of the verb is first, second, or third person singular simply by the form of the suffix on the verb.

For the first person, you can expect –*e* as the suffix
For the second person, you can expect either -*est* or –*ast* as the suffix
For the third person, you can expect either -*eþ* or -*aþ* as the suffix

1st, "I"   -e
2nd, "you"   -est, -ast
3rd, "he/she/it"   -eþ, -aþ

For each of the following verb forms, identify whether the subject will be *I, you* (singular), or *he/she/it.* The first is completed for you as an example.

A. (from *andswarian,* 'to answer') andswarast   *2nd, "you"*
B. (from *fremman,* 'to accomplish') fremest   _____
C. fremeþ   _____
D. fremme   _____
E. (from *lufian,* 'to love') lufast   _____
F. lufaþ   _____
G. (from *leornian,* 'to learn') leornaþ   _____
H. leornast   _____
I. leornie   _____
J. (from *macian,* 'to make') macaþ   _____
K. macast   _____
L. macie   _____
M. (from *werian,* 'to defend') werie   _____
N. werest   _____
O. wereþ   _____

1-6. Lexicon

Although there are some borrowings into OE from Latin, especially in the domain of the Christian religion, there are fewer borrowings than there might have been because speakers of OE tended to use compounds of native words rather than borrowings in many circumstances.

The following are compound words in OE that would eventually be replaced by later borrowings. Match the OE compound to the later borrowing. If you are not familiar with the terms, you should consult a dictionary. The first has been completed for you as an example.

A. fullwihtbæþ   'baptism' + 'bath'   *baptismal font*

B. godcundnes   'god' + 'like' + 'ness'   _____

C. godspellere   'good' + 'news' + 'one, doer'   _____

D. heofoncund   'heaven' + 'like'   _____

E. heofonhlaf   'heaven' + 'bread'   _____

F. tungolwitega   'star' + 'wise man'   _____

G. hlāfgang   'bread' + 'going'   _____

H. ðrōwung   'suffering'   _____

I. ðrōwiendhād   'suffering' + 'condition'   _____

J. ðrōwungrǣdung   'suffering' + 'reading'   _____

K. ānhrān   'one' + 'horn'   _____

L. ġecyðnes   'made known' + 'ness'   _____

astronomer   martyrdom
baptismal font   martyrology
celestial   partaking of the Eucharist
divinity   passion
evangelist   testament
manna   unicorn

1-7. Writing Old English

Learning the basic forms in which you can expect to find the letters of a text in Old English will greatly assist you in approaching an actual manuscript text.

Below are the basic forms you can expect for letters in most texts written in Old English.

Old English alphabet

Aɑ	Ææ	Bƀ	Cᴄ	Dᴅ	Đᵹ	Ee	Fꝼ	Ᵹꝥ	ħh	Iı	Ll
a	ash	be	c	de	eth	e	eff	yogh	há	i	ell
a	æ	b	c	d	ð	e	f	ᴣ (g)	h	i	l

Mm	Nn	Oo	Pp	Rꞃ	Sꞅꞅ	Tᴛ	Uu	Ᵽᵽ	Xx	Yẏ	Þþ
emm	enn	o	pe	err	ess	te	u	wynn	eks	yr	thorn
m	n	o	p	r	s	t	u	p (w)	x	y	þ

http://www.omniglot.com/writing/oldenglish.htm

1. Practice these letter forms. Pay special attention to the letters that no longer exist in the PDE alphabet.

   _____

   _____

   _____

   _____

2. Try writing your name.

   _____

PART TWO: INTERMEDIATE EXERCISES

2-1. The Demonstrative Determiner: *se, þæt, sēo*[1]

		Singular		Plural
	Masc	Neut	Fem	All genders
Nom	se	þæt	sēo	þā
Gen	þæs	þæs	þǣre	þāra
Dat	þǣm, þām	þǣm, þām	þǣre	þǣm, þām
Acc	þone	þæt	þā	þā

Review the forms of the demonstrative determiner provided above and answer the following questions. The first has been completed for you as an example.

A. Which two forms end in *–re*?
    þǣre, feminine genitive singular
    and *þǣre, feminine dative singular*

B. Which two forms end in *–s*?
    _____ and _____

C. Which form ends in *–ne*?
    _____

D. Which forms end in *–m*?
    _____, _____, and _____

E. Which forms end in *–ra*?
    _____

F. In the neuter singular, which two cases have identical forms?
    _____ and _____

G. In the feminine singular, which two cases have identical forms?
    _____ and _____

---

1 You will recall from the discussion in the textbook that these forms were intermediate between demonstrative and definite article senses.

H. In the plural, which two cases have identical forms?

_____ and _____

I. The feminine accusative singular form is identical to which plural forms?

_____ and _____

2-2. Transferring Patterns

The patterns you have identified above are actually fairly reliable and apply to the forms of the other demonstrative as well as the forms of the strong adjective. Your knowledge of those patterns should help you to fill in the missing forms of the proximal demonstrative (*this, these* in PDE) in the paradigm below.

For example, based on the pattern of the distal demonstrative, we notice that the neuter singular form is identical in the nominative and accusative cases. Since here the accusative form is provided for the neuter singular, we can surmise that the nominative singular will be identical, and supply, in the first blank, the form þis.

		Singular		Plural
	Masc	Neut	Fem	All Genders
Nom	þes	A. *þis*	þēos	þās
Gen	B. _____	þisses	C. _____	þissa
Dat	þissum	D. _____	þisse	E._____
Acc	þisne	þis	F. _____	G._____

2-3. The Strong Adjective

Note that the forms of the strong adjective follow the patterns identified above in the distal demonstrative.

Strong forms

	Singular				Plural	
	Masc	Neut	Fem	Masc	Neut	Fem
Nom	*til*	*til*	*tilu*	*tile*	*tilu*	*tila,tile*
Gen	tiles	tiles	tilre	tilra	tilra	tilra
Dat	tilum	tilum	tilre	tilum	tilum	tilum
Acc	*tilne*	*til*	*tile*	*tile*	*tilu*	*tila,tile*

Change the following forms of the strong adjective to distal demonstratives.

For example: til**re** stowe   **þǣre** stowe

Note that the *–re* on the strong adjective form is indicating that the adjective agrees with a singular feminine noun in the genitive or dative case. The *–re* on the demonstrative likewise indicates that the demonstrative agrees with a singular feminine noun in the genitive or dative case.

The first is completed for you as an example.

A. <u>tiles</u> hundes   *þæs*

B. <u>gōdne</u> hund   _____

C. <u>cwicra</u> wifa   _____

D. <u>strangum</u> huntum (pl)   _____

E. <u>strangum</u> huntan (sg)   _____

F. <u>cwicre</u> nædran   _____

G. <u>tilne</u> huntan   _____

H. <u>gōdra</u> wifa   _____

I. <u>gōdum</u> wifum (pl)   _____

J. <u>gōdum</u> wife (sg)   _____

2-4. Noun Exercises

Consider the following paradigms for *hund, wīf, lār,* and *hunta* and answer the questions that follow.

<u>*hund* ("dog") is a strong masculine noun</u>

	Singular	Plural
Nom	hund	hundas
Gen	hundes	hunda
Dat	hunde	hundum
Acc	hund	hundas

<u>*wīf* ("woman") is a strong neuter noun</u>

	Singular	Plural
Nom	wīf	wīf
Gen	wīfes	wīfa
Dat	wīfe	wīfum
Acc	wīf	wīf

lār ("teaching") is a strong feminine noun

	Singular	Plural
Nom	lār	lāre, lāra
Gen	lāre	lāra
Dat	lāre	lārum
Acc	lāre	lāre, lāra

hunta ("hunter") is a weak masculine noun

	Singular	Plural
Nom	hunta	huntan
Gen	huntan	huntena
Dat	huntan	huntum
Acc	huntan	huntan

A. When you encounter the suffix _-es_ on an Old English noun, what would you conclude is its case? _____

B. When you encounter the suffix _-as_ on an Old English noun, what would you conclude is its number? _____

C. When you encounter the suffix _–um_ on an Old English noun, what would you conclude is its number? _____

2-5. Morphology in the Noun Phrase

You will remember that a few of the forms of the demonstratives can signal more than one case, or more than one number.

While _þone_ can only be singular accusative, _þām_ can be singular or plural dative. Use the noun paradigms above as well as your understanding of agreement to identify the following phrases as singular or plural.

The first is completed for you as an example.

	Singular or Plural
A. þām huntan	_Singular_ (while _þām_ can be dative singular or dative plural, _huntan_, if it is dative, must be singular)
B. þām huntum	_____
C. þām hunde	_____
D. þām hundum	_____

E. þām wife _____

F. þām wifum _____

G. þā hundas _____

H. þǣre lāre _____

2-6. Nouns in Context

The following is a passage from Aelfric's *Life of Edmund*. Edmund was an East Anglian king killed by the Great Army as it conquered territories of the Heptarchy in the late 9th century. We have glossed the passage below each line. Answer the questions about the bolded nouns that follow the passage. The first is completed for you as an example.

Keep in mind as you work through this exercise that, as we say in the textbook, the case of the object of most prepositions is dative, but for some it is accusative.

A. Hit ġelamp þā æt nīehstan þæt **þā Deniscan lēode** fērdon
It happened then at last that the Danish people set out

B. mid **sciphere** herġiende and slēande wīde ġeond land, swā
with a fleet ravaging and attacking far and wide throughout (the) land, just

C. swā hira ġewuna is. On **þǣm flotan** wǣron þā fyrmestan
as their custom is. On the ship were the foremost

D. hēafodmenn Hinguar and Hubba, ġeānlæhte þurh **dēofol**, and
leaders Hinguar and Hubba, united through devil, and
hīe on Norþhymbra-lande ġelendon mīd æscum, and āwēston
they in land of the Northumbrians landed with spears, and laid waste

E. **þæt land**, and þā lēode ofslōgon. Þā ġewende Hinguar ēast
that land, and the people slew. Then turned Hinguar east

F. mid his **scipum**, and Hubba belāf on Norþhymbra-lande,
with his ships, and Hubba remained behind in land of the Northumbrians,

G. ġewunnenum siġe mid **wælhrēonesse**. Hinguar þā becōm
winning victory with bloodthirstiness. Hinguar then came
tō Ēast-englum rōwende on þǣm ġeare þe Ælfred æþeling ān
to East Anglia rowing in the year that Alfred prince one

H. and twentiġ ġeara wæs, sē þe **West-seaxna** cyning siþþan wearþ
and twenty years was, he who of the West Saxons king since became

I. mære. And **se foresægda Hinguar** færliċe, swā swā wulf, on
    famous.   And   the aforesaid   Hinguar   suddenly,   just as   a wolf,   on

J. land bestealcode, and **þā lēode** slōg, **weras** and **wīf**   and þā
    land   moved stealthily,   and   the people   slew,   men   and   women and   the

    unwittigan ċild,   and tō bismere tūcode   þā bilewitan crīstenan.
    ignorant   children, and   shamefully   tormented   the innocent   Christians.

A. Why is the phrase **þā Deniscan lēode** is in the nominative case? That is, what is
    its function in the sentence?
    þā Deniscan lēode is the subject of the verb fērdon

B. Why is the noun **sciphere** in the dative? That is, what is its function in the sen-
    tence? (note that *mid* is a preposition)
    _____

C. Why is the phrase **þæm flotan** in the dative? That is, what is its function in the
    sentence?
    _____

D. Why is **dēofol** in the accusative?
    _____

E. Why is **þæt land** in the accusative?
    _____

F. Why is the noun **scipum** in the dative?
    _____

G. Why is the noun **wælhrēonesse** in the dative?
    _____

H. Why is the noun **West-seaxna** in the genitive?
    _____

I. Why is the phrase **se foresægda Hinguar** in the nominative?
    _____

J. Why are the nouns **lēode**, **weras**, and **wīf** in the accusative?
    _____

2-7. Reading and Writing in Runes

Although literacy in the Old English period focused on Latin and was based on the Roman alphabet, the set of alphabetic symbols from the Germanic world remained accessible in the Old English period, and scribes sometimes embedded signatures into manuscripts with runic letters or integrated runic symbols into other kinds of texts. A number of runic inscriptions also survive from the Old English period. These inscriptions are of interest in part because they link the Anglo-Saxons to their Germanic past and suggest ongoing connection at least to an idea of that past.

The following is one set of runic symbols available during the OE period. Note that each symbol has a name and that each symbol can represent a sound but also the word that is its name.

rune								
name	feoh	ur	thorn	os	rad	cen	gyfu	wynn
translation	cattle	ox	thorn	god	road	torch	gift	joy
transliteration	<f>	<u>	<th>	<o>	<r>	<c>	<g>	<w>
name	haegl	nyd	is	gear	eoh	peord	eolhx	sigel
translation	hail	affliction	ice	year	yew	unknown	elk's	sun
transliteration	<h>	<n>	<i>	<j, g> [j, g]	<ī, ȝ>	<p> ?	x	<s>
name	tir	beorc	eh (eoh)	mann	lagu	Ing	eðel	dæg
translation	Tyr, Tiw	birch	horse	man	lake	Ing	homeland	dat
transliteration	<t>	<b>	<e>	<m>	<l>	[ŋ]	<oe, e>	<d>
name	ac	ash	yr	iar,ior	ear			
translation	oak	ash	horn? bow?	eel?	earth			
transliteration	<a>	<æ>	<y>	<ia>	<ea>			

A. Write your name in runes as closely as you can, given the sounds represented by runes. The spelling of some names may be straightforward; others not. For example, names like Sharon may have to begin with the rune for the sound [s].

_____

B. What do you notice about these letter shapes? How are they different from the shapes of the Roman letters you usually use?

_____

2-8. Languages in Contact

As you know, the Anglo-Saxons approached literacy through the Church, and thus through the language of the Church, Latin. They were conscious of the differences between Latin and Old English on many levels, and they wrestled sometimes with how to translate from Latin into English with the greatest accuracy, as well as with how to write in English, with Latin as the model of how a language "should" work.

Consider the following passage from Ælfric's Preface to Genesis, in which Ælfric explicitly argues for a method of translation from Latin to English. A translation follows the Old English text.

Nū ys sēo foresǣde bōc on manegum stōwum swīðe nearolīce gesett, and þēah swīðe dēoplīce on þām gāstlīcum andgite, and hēo is swā geendebyrd swā swā God silf hig gedihte þām wrītere Moise, and wē durron nā māre āwrītan on Englisc þonne þæt Lēden hæfð, nē þā endebirdnisse āwendan būton þām ānum, þæt þæt Lēden and þæt Englisc nabbað nā āne wīsan on þǣre sprǣce fandunge. Ǣfre sē þe āwent oððe sē þe tǣcð of Lēdene on Englisc, ǣfre hē sceal gefadian hit swā þæt þæt Englisc hæbbe his āgene wīsan, elles hit bið swīðe gedwolsum tō rǣdenne þām þe þæs Lēdenes wīsan ne can. Is ēac tō witene þæt sume gedwolmen wǣron þe woldon āwurpan þā ealdan ǣ, and sume woldon habban þā ealdan and āwurpan þā nīwan, swā þā Iūdēiscean dōð; ac Crīst sylf and his apostolas ūs tǣhton ǣgðer tō healdenne þā ealdan gāstlīce and þā nīwan sōðlīce mid weorcum. God gescēop ūs twā ēagan and twā ēaran, twā nosðirlu, twēgen weleras, twā handa and twegen fēt, and hē wolde ēac habban twā gecȳðnissa on þissere worulde gesett, þā ealdan and þā nīwan; for þām þe hē dēð swā swā hine silfne gewyrð, and hē nǣnne rǣdboran næfð, nē nān man ne þearf him cweðan tō, 'Hwī dēst ðū swā?' Wē sceolon āwendan ūrne willan tō his gesetnissum, and wē ne magon gebīgean his gesetnissa on ūrum lustum.

Now, the aforementioned book is very narrowly composed in many places, and nevertheless very deeply in the spiritual sense, and is put in order just as God himself dictated to Moses, and we dare not write in English more than that which Latin has, nor change the order except in one way, in that Latin and English do not have one and the same way in the experiencing of speech. He who translates or he who teaches from Latin into English must always try to make it so that the English has its own manner, or else it will be very misleading to read for anyone who does not know the Latin. It is also to be known that there were certain misled people who wished to cast down the old law, and certain who wished to have the old and cast down the new, as the Jews do.

But Christ himself and his apostles taught us to hold to the old law in a spiritual sense, and to the new law truly in deeds. God shaped for us two eyes

and two ears, two nostrils, two lips, two hands, and two feet, and he wished also to have two testaments established in this world, the old and the new; because he does as it pleases him, and he does not have any advisor, nor does any man have need to say to him, "Why did you do thus?" We must turn our will to his laws, and we may not bend his laws to our desires.
(text from *Bright's Anglo-Saxon Reader.* https://en.wikisource.org/wiki/ Bright%27s_Anglo-Saxon_Reader/Ælfric%27s_Preface_to_Genesis Accessed March 17, 2019. Translation is our own.)

A. What is Ælfric's position on how translation of Scripture from Latin into English should progress?

_____

_____

_____

_____

B. How important is it to keep words in the same order as you translate?

_____

_____

_____

_____

C. When is it necessary to change the order of the words?

_____

_____

_____

_____

D. How does Ælfric make the idea of having two different versions of a biblical text (one in Latin and one in English) seem both natural and divinely ordained?

_____

_____

_____

_____

PART THREE: ADVANCED EXERCISES

3-1. More Nouns

Consider the following forms of strong and weak nouns in Old English.

hund ("dog") is a strong masculine noun

	Singular	Plural
Nom	hund	hundas
Gen	hundes	hunda
Dat	hunde	hundum
Acc	hund	hundas

hunta ("hunter") is a weak masculine noun

	Singular	Plural
Nom	hunta	huntan
Gen	huntan	huntena
Dat	huntan	huntum
Acc	huntan	huntan

nædre ("serpent") is a weak feminine noun

	Singular	Plural
Nom	nædre	nædran
Gen	nædran	nædrena
Dat	nædran	nædrum
Acc	nædran	nædran

wīf ("woman") is a strong neuter noun

	Singular	Plural
Nom	wīf	wīf
Gen	wīfes	wīfa
Dat	wīfe	wīfum
Acc	wīf	wīf

lār ("teaching") is a strong feminine noun

	Singular	Plural
Nom	lār	lāre, lāra
Gen	lāre	lāra
Dat	lāre	lārum
Acc	lāre	lāre, lāra

mann ("person") is a masculine mutation plural

	Singular	Plural
Nom	mann	menn
Gen	mannes	manna
Dat	menn	mannum
Acc	mann	menn

Now, consider the following excerpt from an Old English remedy for headache:

ġif mannes hēafod tōbrocen sīe,   (line 1)
If   a man's   head   broken   is,

ġenim þā wyrte betonican, ...   (line 2)
take   the herb   betony,

þiġe hīe þonne on hātum bēore.   (line 3)
drink it   then   in hot   beer.

Þonne hãlað þæt hēafod swyðe hraðe.   (line 4)
Then   heals   that head   very   quickly.

Perform the following changes to this recipe. The first is completed for you as an example.

A. *cnapa* (m.) "boy," "servant": *cnapa* is a weak masculine noun like *hunta*.
   What form of the word *cnapa* would you use if you were treating a boy instead of a man? That is, substitute the appropriate form of *cnapa* for the word *mannes* in line 1.
   cnapan (genitive singular)

B. *widuwe* (f.) "widow": *widuwe* is a weak feminine noun like *nædre*.
   What form of the word *widuwe* would you use if you were treating a widow with a headache? That is, substitute the appropriate form of *widuwe* for *mannes* in line 1.

   _____

C. *earm* (m.) "arm": *earm* is a strong masculine noun like *hund*.
   What form of *earm* would you use if you were treating an arm instead of a head in line 1?

   _____

D. What form of *earm* would you use if you were treating an arm instead of a head in line 4?

   _____

E. Review the forms of the demonstrative *se, þæt, sēo* given in exercise 2-1. If you changed the noun *hēafod* to the noun *earm* in line 4, note that you would have to change *þæt* to the form of the demonstrative that agrees with *earm*. What would that form be?

_____

F. *meolc* (f.) "milk": *meolc* is a strong feminine noun like *lār*.
    What form of *meolc* would you use in line 3 if you were soaking the herb in milk instead of beer?

_____

G. Review the forms of the strong adjective given in exercise 2-3, and in Chapter Seven of the textbook. If you changed the noun *bēor* to the noun *meolc*, note that you would have to change the form of the adjective *hāt* so that it agreed with *meolc*. What would that form of *hāt* be?

_____

H. Integrate the changes above into the paragraph.

ġif mannes hēafod tōbrocen sīe,	ġif _____ _____ tōbrocen sīe
If a man's head broken is,	If a boy's arm
ġenim þā wyrte betonican, ...	ġenim þā wyrte betonican,
take the herb betony,	take the herb betony,
þiġe hīe þonne on hātum bēore.	þiġe hīe þonne on _____ _____
drink it then in hot beer.	drink it then in hot milk
Þonne hālað þæt hēafod swyðe hraðe.	Þonne hālað _____ _____ swyðe hraðe.
Then heals that head very quickly.	Then heals that arm very quickly

3-2. Nouns and Agreement

Fill in the blanks in the following sentences with nouns from exercise 3-1 (*mann, cnapa, widuwe, hund, hunta, hēafod, earm, meolc, bēor, nædre, wīf*) that agree with the forms of the demonstrative provided. The first is completed for you as an example.

For example:
Do you see that _____?
A. þone *hund* ġesiehst þū?

That _____ gave that _____ to that _____
B. Se _____ ġeaf þæt _____ to þǣm _____.
C. Þæt _____ ġeaf þone_____ to þǣre _____.

That _____ was good.

D. Sēo _____ wæs tilu.

E. Se _____ wæs til.

That _____'s dog was swift.

F. Ðæs _____ hund wæs swift.

G. Ðǣre _____ hund wæs swift.

I love that _____!

H. Iċ lufiġe þæt _____!

I. Iċ lufiġe þā _____!

That _____ lufode that _____.

J. Se _____ lufode þone _____.

K. Seo _____ lufode þæt _____.

3-3. Reading Old English

The following passages are from the Old English *Life of Saint Margaret* in which the saint faces a dragon and then a devil. Use your knowledge of the forms of the determiner *se, sēo, þæt* as well as the third person pronouns and identify the likely cases for the underlined phrases. The paradigms are provided below.

Forms of the Demonstrative Determiner

| | Singular | | Plural | |
	Masc	Neut	Fem	All Genders
Nom	se	þæt	sēo	þā
Gen	þæs	þæs	þǣre	þāra
Dat	þǣm, þām	þǣm, þām	þǣre	þǣm, þām
Acc	þone	þæt	þā	þā

Forms of the Third Person Personal Pronoun

| | Singular | | Plural | |
	Masc	Neut	Fem	All Genders
Nom	hē	hit	hēo	hīe
Gen	his	his	hire	hira
Dat	him	him	hire	him
Acc	hine	hit	hīe	hīe

In the following exercise, identify the case of the underlined noun phrases in the passage. After you have identified the cases for the underlined phrases, translate the passages with the gloss provided and your knowledge of these few words. Note that in this passage we have not marked the long vowels or used the <ġ>. This is often how Old English texts will appear in non-beginner editions! The first has been completed for you as an example.

deofol: devil
draca: dragon
fæmne: woman
halig: holy (note that in forms with a suffix the -i- is lost)
locc: lock (of hair)

A. **Se draca sette his muþ ofer þære halgan fæmnan heafod**
         set   mouth   head

   se draca *nominative*
   þære halgan fæmnan *genitive or dative*
   Translation: *The dragon set his mouth over the head of the holy woman.*

B. **and hie forswealh.**
            swallowed

   hie _____
   Translation: _____

C. **Ac seo halge Margareta worhte Cristes rodetacen**
     But   made   Christ's   cross-sign

   seo halge Margareta _____
   Translation: _____

D. **innan þæs dracan innoþe.**
     inside   belly

   þæs dracan_____
   Translation: _____

E. **Seo hine toslat on twegen dælas**
              split   into two   parts

   seo_____
   hine_____
   Translation: _____

F. And <u>seo halge fæmne</u> eode
        went

seo halge fæmne _____

Translation: _____

ut of þæs dracan innoþe ungewæmmed.
out of the   dragon's   belly   unstained

G. And <u>se deofol</u> uparas.
              rose up

se deofol _____

Translation: _____

H. Seo halge Margareta gegrap <u>þone deofol</u> be <u>þæm locce</u>
                               grasped   by

þone deofol _____

þæm locce _____

Translation: _____

I. And <u>hine</u> on eorþan awearp
                     earth   cast down

hine_____

Translation: _____

J. And <u>his</u> swyþran eage utastang
              right   eye   put out

his_____

Translation: _____

K. And ealle his ban tobrysde,
        all   bones burst,

And sette <u>hire</u> swyþran fot ofer his swyran
        set   right   foot   neck

hire _____

Translation: _____

L. And <u>him</u> to cwæð:
              said

him _____

Translation: _____

"Gewit fram minum mægþhade!"
"Get away from   my   maidenhood!"

3-4. Working with the Strong Verbs

The strong verbs indicate changes in the principal parts by gradations in the stem vowel. There are 7 classes of strong verbs in OE.

The principal parts of the strong verbs are the infinitive, the simple past 3rd singular, the simple past plural, and the past participle.

For **Class 1 strong verbs**, the vowels of the principal parts are the following:

ī, ā, i, i

This means that for the sample verb *rīdan* (to ride)
the infinitive, **rīdan**, will have an "ī" in the stem.
the simple past 3rd person singular form, **rād**, will have an "ā" in the stem.
the simple past plural, **ridon**, will have an "i" in the stem.
the past participle, **riden**, will have an "i" in the stem.

Several Class 1 strong verbs follow.

Infinitive (ī)	Past 3rd sing (ā)	Past pl (i)	Past part (i)
bīdan (to await)	bād	bidon	biden
wrītan (to write)	wrāt	writon	writen
ġewītan (to depart)	ġewāt	ġewiton	ġewiten
bītan (to bite)	bāt	biton	biten

Given the forms in each set, fill in the remaining principal parts for these Class 1 strong verbs. The first row has been completed for you as an example.

	PDE	infinitive form	past. 3rd per sg.	past. plural form	past participle
A.	to cease	swīcan	swāc	swicon	swicen
B.	to touch			hrinon	
C.	to cut	snīþan			
D.	to ascend				stigen

Class 2 strong verbs follow the pattern
    ēo, ēa, u, o   or   ū, ēa, u, o

Infinitive (ēo/ū)	Past 3rd sing (ēa)	Past pl (u)	Past part (o)
bēodan(to command)	bēad	budon	boden
drēogan (to endure)	drēag	drugon	drogen
cēosan (to choose)	cēas	curon	coren
frēosan (to freeze)	frēas	fruron	froren
brūcan (to enjoy)	brēac	brucon	brocen
būgan (to bow)	bēag	bugon	bogen

Exercise:
Given the following forms for Class 2 strong verbs, generate the remaining principal parts.

	PDE	infinitive form	past. 3rd per sg.	past. plural form	past participle
E.	to push	scūfan	scēaf		
F.	to bow	lūtan			
G.	to smoke	smēocan			smocen
H.	to rue	hrēowan		hruwon	

Questions
I.   Which strong verb class will have an "ā" in the 3rd past singular? _____
J.   Which strong verb class will have an "i" in the past plural? _____
K.   Which strong verb class will have a "ū" in the infinitive? _____
L.   Which strong verb class will have an "ēo" in the infinitive? _____

Identify the Class 1 or 2 strong verb forms in the following sentences. The first is completed for you as an example.

M. Abraham **arās** on þǣre ilcan nihte. (from arīsan, "to arise")
    Abraham   arose   on   that   same   night.

   The verb is a Class 1 strong verb (note the sequence ī, ā)

N. Leofstan **rād** tō þām halgan. (from rīdan, "to ride")
    Leofstan   rode   to the   holy man.

O. Se hwæl Jonah up **aspāw**. (from aspīwan, "to spew")
    The whale   Jonah   spewed up.

_____

P. He **bēad**   ðæt ælc man swa dōn sceolde. (from bēodan, "to command")
    He commanded that each man so do must.

_____

Q. Hīe yfeles **geswicon**. (from ġeswīcan, "to cease from")
    They from evil ceased.

_____

R. On ðām seofoðan dæge, God ġeendode his weorc,
    On the seventh   day,   God ended   his work,
    and **ġeswāc** þā, and ġehalgode ðone seofoðan dæge. (from ġeswīcan, "to cease from")
    and rested   then, and hallowed   the   seventh   day.

_____

S. In R. above, you have identified the form *ġeswāc*, a form of a strong verb. Note that there are two other verb forms in that sentence, *ġeendode*, and *ġehalgode*, forms of *ġeendian* and *ġehalgian* respectively. Are *ġeendian* and *ġehalgian* strong or weak verbs?

_____

3-5. Old English Syntax

Bruce Mitchell and Fred C. Robinson identify correlation as one characteristic of Old English syntax that "makes us feel that OE is a foreign language" (*A Guide to Old English*, 8th ed. [Malden, MA: Wiley-Blackwell, 2012], 68). Furthermore, as Mitchell and Robinson also observe, as an additional difficulty for learners of Old English, a number of correlative pairs exist in OE in which the adverb and the subordinating conjunction have the same form. *Þā*, for example, can be translated into PDE as either "when" or "then," *þǣr* can be translated as either "there" or "where," and *þider* can be translated as either "thither" or "whither." But close attention to the syntax in sentences using these pairs can provide us with fairly reliable clues as to when to translate a form as the conjunction and when to translate it as the adverb.

Consider the following examples:

Eft þa þa God com and hie gehierdon his stefne...þa behydde Adam hine...(Genesis)
Afterwards when God came and they heard   his voice   then hid   Adam himself

Eft þa on fyrste, æfter fela gearu, þa seo hergung geswac and sib wearð forgifen
Afterwards, in a while,   after   a few years,   when the harrying   ceased   and peace was   given

þam geswenctan folce, þa fengon hi togædere and worhton ane cyrcan...
to the harassed   people, then joined   they together   and   made   a   church

(Aelfric, *Life of Edmund*)

Þa ic ða gemunde hu sio lar Lædengeðiodes
When I then remembered   how the   teaching of Latin

ær ðissum afeallen wæs giond Angelcynne
before this   fallen off   was   throughout England

ða ongan ic ongemang oðrum mislicum and manigfealdum bisgum ðisses kynerices
then undertook I among   the many various   and manifold   cares   of this   kingdom

ða boc wendan on English...(Alfred, Preface to *Pastoral Care*)
this book   to translate   into English

Þa se cyning Þa Þas word gehyrde, Þa answarode he him...(Bede, *Conversion of Edwin*)
When the king   then those words   heard,   then answered   he them...

A. What is the order in which the subject and verb occur when *þa* is likely translated as "when"?

_____

B. What is the order in which the subject and verb occur when *þa* is likely translated as "then"?

_____

C. We can now formulate a rule to help predict when *þa* will be translated as the conjuction and when it will be translated as the adverb.

    þa followed by the order SV is translated _____
    þa followed by the order VS is translated _____

D. But note that this rule will not hold in much of the poetry, and that it is more likely to appear in texts that are translated into Old English from Latin. Why do you think this is the case?

_____

_____

_____

_____

3-6. Writing Old English

Review, if necessary, the introduction to the basic Old English letter forms in exercise 1-7 of this workbook chapter. In addition, keep the following things in mind:

While the Anglo-Saxons tended not to use the letters <k> or <q> or <z>, those letter forms were available to them.

A macron over a vowel often indicates that a following <m> or <n> has been omitted.

A thorn with a bar across the ascender is a scribal abbreviation for "þæt."

The symbol that looks like a "7" is an abbreviation for "and."

A. Practice writing the following words in the Old English script you practiced in exercise 1-7.

menn   heofdum   eagan   brade

Be sure to try out each of the possible forms for each letter as you write these words.

B. Below is an excerpt from a late Old English version of a text called *Wonders* (or *Marvels*) *of the East*.

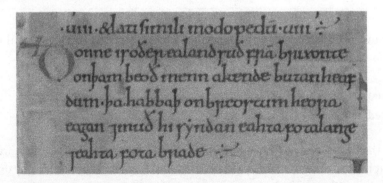

Transliterate, that is, copy this text into the letters of PDE (but do retain <þ> and <ð>). Note that the large first letter is <ð>.

_____

_____

_____

_____

_____

_____

C. Below is an earlier version of the same text. Even though this version of the text is
    damaged, you will be able to recognize a number of the words you have worked
    with above, and you should now be experienced enough to begin to transliterate
    this text as well.

_____

_____

_____

_____

_____

_____

The words you see penned above the text in this version are in a later hand, and as
they helped that later reader make sense of the passage, they reflect changes in the
language that we will return to later in this workbook.

Here is a translation of the passage into PDE.

> *Then there is another island south from Brixontes, on which men are born*
> *without heads. They have on their breasts their eyes and mouth. They are eight*
> *feet tall and eight feet broad.*

Both of these manuscripts contain illustrations. Below are the passages you have
worked with in the context of the whole page on which they appear.

Note that this later manuscript, Cotton Tiberius Bv, contains the text in both Latin and English. The passage we transliterated is the second paragraph in the first column on the left. The text above it, beginning with the <e> is a Latin version of the same text.

The second version we transliterated is from part of Cotton Vitellius Axv, which we now call the *Beowulf* Manuscript, because it also contains our only copy of *Beowulf*.

D. How would you characterize the differences between these two presentations of the text and illustrations?

_____

_____

_____

_____

E. What is the effect of encountering this passage in these two very different
    contexts?

    _____

    _____

    _____

    _____

F. Does the bilingual version suggest a different audience?

    _____

    _____

    _____

    _____

G. Many scholars have characterized the illustrations in the English-only version of
    this text as childish or unskilled. Why might illustrations have seemed important
    enough to include with this text, even if the scribe/illustrator did not possess a
    great deal of technical drawing skill?

    _____

    _____

    _____

    _____

A note on manuscript names:

Different libraries and collections identify manuscripts by different systems. Both
manuscripts discussed above are in the British Library. Their names provide the
following information about their original location in their first known collection.

The word "Cotton" indicates that the manuscripts were once part of the collection
of Sir Robert Cotton.

The words "Vitellius" and "Tiberius" were part of how that library was organized.
Manuscripts were organized underneath sculptures of Roman emperors. The Vitellius manuscript was under the statue of Vitellius. The Tiberius manuscript was under
the statue of Tiberius.

The letter and number that follow each tell us which shelf and how far in from the left on that shelf the manuscript was housed.

Thus, the name BL Cotton Vitellius Axv tells us the manuscript is now part of the collection at the British Library, and that it was once part of the collection of Sir Robert Cotton, shelved under the statue of Vitellius, on the first shelf down, fifteen books in.

Notes

_____

_____

_____

_____

_____

_____

_____

_____

_____

_____

_____

_____

_____

_____

_____

_____

_____

_____

_____

Notes

_____

_____

_____

_____

_____

_____

_____

_____

_____

_____

_____

_____

_____

_____

_____

_____

_____

_____

_____

_____

_____

_____

Chapter Eight

1-1. ME Orthography

Given the following Old English words, provide the likely Middle English spelling for those words. Note that in some cases this change in spelling will reflect a change in the phonology as well. In all instances, the Old English word has been preserved into Present-day English with its spelling generally set in place during the Middle English period. The first is completed for you as an example.

A. ūt   *out*

B. strengð   _____

C. æt   _____

D. sæp   _____

E. bæð   _____

F. riht   _____

G. þing   _____

H. þū   _____

I. hecg   _____

J. tēð   _____

K. liht   _____

L. ċinn   _____

M. ċest   _____

N. fūl   _____

O. scrift   _____

P. scilling   _____

Q. ċildisc   _____

R. flōr   _____

S. wecg   _____

T. sūr   _____

U. cwic   _____

1-2. ME Phonology

One of the features of sound change in ME is the simplification of many consonant clusters from Old English. (See Fernand Mossé, *A Handbook of Middle English*, translated by James A. Walker, Baltimore: The Johns Hopkins UP, 1991.)

For example:

    Rule 1. initial [h] is lost in the combinations [hl], [hn], and [hr]

    Rule 2. [l] is often lost before [tʃ] or after [tʃ] in certain syllables

    Rule 3. [v] before a consonant is lost[1]

    (and the combination [v] + cons may occur after an unstressed vowel has been lost)

Given the following OE words, fill in the consonants you would expect to find in the ME developments of those words. The first is completed for you as an example. (The meanings for each of these words accompany the answers to this exercise.)

A. OE   hrung   ME   _r_unge

B. OE   hnutu   ME   ___ ute

C. OE   hnecca   ME   ___ ekke

D. OE   hroc   ME   ___ ok

E. OE   heafod   ME   he ___

F. OE   hlafdige   ME   ___ avedi but also (consider Rule 3 and that the -e- would be unstressed and eventually lost) ___a___ y

G. OE   hlaford   ME   ___overd but also (consider Rule 3 and that the -e- would be unstressed and eventually lost) ___ ___ord

H. OE   ælċ   ME   e___e

I. OE   swylċ   ME   su___e

J. OE   wenċel   ME   we___e

K. OE   miċel   ME   mu___

---

1 It is important to remember that the letter <v>, although known to the Anglo-Saxons, was not frequently used and instead <f> was used for both [f] and [v].

1-3. ME Phonology and Morphology

Sound changes involving unstressed final sounds at the end of the OE period and during the ME period had significant consequences for the structure of the language. In particular:

Final -n > Ø
Final -m > final -n > Ø
Final -a, -e, -o, -u > ə (spelled <e>) > Ø (often preserved as "-e" in spelling even after the sound is lost)

The following are the paradigms for the OE weak masculine noun *nama* ("name") and the OE strong feminine noun *heall* ("hall"). Beside each form, fill in the form you would expect after these likely sound changes. Note that a single form may pass through several of these changes (final -m > -n > -a > -ə > Ø, for example). When that is the case, we have provided multiple spaces for you to record each stage of the changes. The first is completed for you as an example.

A. Singular Genitive   tungan   >*tunga* (-n > Ø)

                                                               >*tunge* (-a > -ə)

B. Singular Nominative   nama   >_____

C. Singular Genitive   naman   >_____

                                                               >_____

D. Singular Dative   naman   >_____

                                                               >_____

E. Singular Accusative   naman   >_____

                                                               >_____

F. Plural Nominative   naman   >_____

                                                               >_____

G. Plural Genitive   namena   >_____

                                                               >_____

                                                               >_____

H. Plural Dative   namum   >_____

                                                               >_____

                                                                 >_____

I. Plural Accusative   naman   >_____

                                                               >_____

J. Singular Nominative   heall   >_____
K. Singular Genitive   healle   >_____
L. Singular Dative   healle   >_____
M. Singular Accusative   healle   >_____
N. Plural Nominative   healla   >_____
O. Plural Genitive   heallena >_____
                                     >_____
                                     >_____
P. Plural Dative   heallum   >_____
                                     >_____
                                     >_____
Q. Plural Accusative   healla   >_____

R. How many distinct forms of *nama* and *heall* remain after these changes?

_____

S. How do we make those nouns plural and possessive in PDE?

    _____ and _____ in the plural and

    _____ and _____ in the possessive.

Consider the forms of the OE strong masculine noun *gāst* ("spirit"). What happens to those forms if we chart the effects of the same sound changes? (Note that if a suffix does not contain sounds affected by the sound change rules above, you should simply copy the form unchanged.)

T. Singular Nominative   gāst   >_____
U. Singular Genitive   gāstes[2]   >_____
V. Singular Dative   gāste   >_____
W. Singular Accusative   gāst   >_____
X. Plural Nominative   gāstas[3]   >_____
Y. Plural Genitive   gāsta   >_____
Z. Plural Dative   gāstum   >_____
                                       >_____
                                       >_____

---

2 Note that the vowel in the last syllable will also be lost for most varieties of Middle English.
3 Note that the vowel in the last syllable will also be lost for most varieties of Middle English.

AA. Plural Accusative   gāstas   >_____

BB. How many distinct forms of *gāst* remain after these changes?

_____

CC. Where do the plural and possessive suffixes you identified above as the
PDE plural and possessive forms for *name* and *hall* likely come from?

_____

1-4. Languages in Contact: The ME Lexicon

The lexicon of Middle English expands considerably with literally thousands of borrowings from several varieties of French. These borrowings tended to occur in certain predictable domains, however. Those patterns of borrowing are still traceable in the lexicon of PDE.

For each of the following categories, each of which reflects a domain in which we would expect borrowings from French, generate at least five words that fit into that category. Look up the words in the *Oxford English Dictionary*. Note whether the word is native or borrowed, if borrowed from what language, and the year of the first citation.

A. Words that have to do with courts of law

word	native, or borrowed from what language	year
_____	_____	_____
_____	_____	_____
_____	_____	_____
_____	_____	_____
_____	_____	_____

B. Words that have to do with aristocratic and court life (*king, lady, crown* ...)

word	native, or borrowed from what language	year
_____	_____	_____
_____	_____	_____
_____	_____	_____
_____	_____	_____
_____	_____	_____

1-5. External Events of the ME Period

Place the following external events in the order in which they occurred.

A. _____ English victory at the Battle of Stamford Bridge
B. _____ English Peasants' Revolt
C. _____ Black Plague
D. _____ Start of the Hundred Years' War
E. _____ Marriage of Æþelred and Emma
F. _____ Rule of the Danish kings in England
G. _____ Norman Conquest

1-6. Writing in the ME Period

The ME period experiences a significant increase in literacy. Although we tend to think about literacy in terms of reading audiences, and reading for pleasure, in the ME period it is also not only the vast legal and court records, but also the rise of universities that created a demand for rapidly produced texts. And these texts were produced by hand: they were manuscripts not printed materials. Not surprisingly, styles of writing changed to accommodate the need for speed.

Many students today do not learn cursive writing in elementary school. One justification provided for no longer teaching cursive writing is that many students no longer need to write quickly by hand. For the most part, students now tend to use one or another kind of keyboard rather than writing by hand. For this reason, the immediate difference between styles of writing close to what we call "printing" (like the handwriting we examined in the previous chapter) and cursive may seem less intuitively about speed.

A. Just to get a sense of the difference, try "printing" the following sentence with attention to writing as clearly as possible:

The young student consulted the astrolabe.

_____

Note that if you are "printing" carefully, each time you make a new letter you must lift your pen, and for some letters, like <t>, you must first write the vertical line then lift your pen and replace it to construct the horizontal bar, then lift it again to start the next letter.

B. How many times did you have to lift your pen to write the word "consulted"?

_____

C. Try "printing" the same sentence as you might with your usual style of printing, and as if you were in a hurry or taking notes during a lecture.

_____

D. What is the difference between the two "printed" sentences that you generated? You might say one is "messier" than the other, but try to be more specific. How are the letter shapes different?

_____

E. Are there connections between letters? _____

F. Here is the same sentence in cursive. Either write the sentence in cursive, if you learned it, or trace the cursive model here.

The young student consulted the astrolabe.

_____

Cursive styles of writing enable you to write longer segments without lifting your pen. One reason cursive looks "loopy" is that the introduction of loops helps to connect letters and reduce pen lift (Raymond Clemens and Timothy Graham, *Introduction to Manuscript Studies*, Ithaca: Cornell UP, 2007: 160). If you are writing cursive, the word "young," for example, does not require you to lift your pen at all for the entire word.

G. How many times did you have to lift your pen to write the word "consulted" in cursive? _____

Although cursive scripts had been used in the early Middle Ages, after a long period of disuse, England was one of the earliest European countries to re-introduce cursive script beginning in the late 12th century (Michelle Brown, *A Guide to Western Historical Scripts from Antiquity to 1600* [London: The British Library, 1990, repr. 1999], 80), and it developed that script in the 13th century into a distinctive script called "cursiva anglicana."

PART TWO: INTERMEDIATE EXERCISES

2-1. ME Phonology

In exercise 1-2 we considered some consonant simplifications. But we can also trace the addition of some consonants in certain environments. (See Fernand Mossé, *A Handbook of Middle English*, trans. James A. Walker [Baltimore: The Johns Hopkins UP, 1991].)

1. [d] between [n] and [l] or [r]
2. [p] between [m] and [t]
3. [b] between [m] and [l] and after final [m]
4. [t] between [s] and [n] and after final [n] or [s]

Given the following OE, Old French, or Middle Low German words, fill in the consonants you would expect to find in the ME developments of those words. In a few instances we have listed, instead of a source, a variant of a ME word.

A.	OE spinel	ME spi_____ e
B.	OE þunor	ME thu_____ re
C.	OE æmtiġ	ME e_____y
D.	OE behæs	ME behe_____
E.	Old French ancien	ME auncie_____
F.	Old French tiran	ME tyrau_____
G.	OE bremel	ME bre_____e
H.	OE þymel	ME thi_____e
I.	Middle Low German tumeler	ME tu_____er
J.	OE þuma	ME thu_____ (Note that the final -*a* will be dropped and thus the word ends in -*m* which will trigger the addition of a new final consonant.)

2-2. From OE to ME

The following are passages from the Bible in OE. As you review some of the changes that occur in English between OE and ME, see if you can predict what some of the options might have been for the translators of the same passage into ME. (OE and ME passages are taken from A.G. Rigg, ed. *The English Language: A Historical Reader* [New York: Appleton-Century-Crofts, 1968].)

OE Passage One

Ða andswarode him Petrus, and cwæð,

Then answered   them Peter,   and   said,

"Drihten, gyf þu hyt eart, hat me cuman to þe ofer þas wæteru. (Matthew 14:28)

"Lord,   if   you   it   are,   order me   to come   to you over   these waters.

Review the following changes that occur from OE to ME. (Also see the Chapter Eight in the textbook.) Fill in the blanks for the ME change. The first is completed for you as an example.

A. Orthography: OE   ME

               <þ>   *<th>*

               <u> (for /u:/)   _____

               <e> (for /e:/)   _____

B. Phonology: OE   ME

               /æ/   _____

               final -n   _____

               final vowel   _____

C. Morphology: OE   ME

               Many possible

               plural inflections

               for nouns   _____

D. Syntax: OE   ME

               Adv VS   _____

Given your knowledge of these changes, fill in the likely forms in ME for the following words that occur in Passage One above. The first is completed for you as an example.

E. Orthography: OE   ME

               þu   *thou*   (You noted above, in A. that <þ> was replaced by <th> during the ME period, and that long <u> was replaced by <ou>.)

               þe   _____

F. Phonology: OE   ME

wæteru _____

cuman _____

G. Morphology: OE   ME

wæteru _____

H. Syntax: OE   ME

Đa andswarode him Petrus   _____
Then answered   him   Peter

While of course translation decisions cannot *simply* reflect general changes in the language, the late ME translation of the Bible provides the following for this passage, much of which you likely predicted above!

ME Passage One
And Petre answeride, and seide, "Lord, if thou art, comaunde me to come to thee on the watris."

OE Passage Two

Đa geopenode Noe ðæs arces hrof, and beheold ut
Then opened   Noah the   ark's   roof, and looked   out

and geseah ðæt ðære eorðan bradnis wæs adruwod (Genesis 8:13)
and saw   that   the   earth's   broadness was   dried up

As you did for Passage One, review the following changes from OE to ME. (Also see Chapter Eight in the textbook.) Fill in the blanks for the ME change.

I. Orthography: OE   ME

ð> _____

<o> (for /o:/) _____

J. Phonology: OE   ME

/æ/ _____

h before r _____

K. Morphology and syntax: OE   ME

                                 inflected genitive _____

                                 demonstrative determiner _____

L. Syntax: OE   ME

               Adv VS   _____

Given your knowledge of these changes, fill in the likely forms in ME for the following words that occur in OE Passage Two.

M. Orthography: OE   ME

                  ðæt   _____

                  hrof   _____

N. Phonology: OE   ME

                wæs   _____

O. Morphology and syntax: OE   ME

                        ðæs arces _____

                        the   ark's

                        ðære eorðan _____

                        the   earth's

P. Syntax: OE   ME

               Ða geopenode Noe _____

               Then opened   Noah

The ME translation of this passage follows:
ME Passage Two
And Noe opened the roof of the schip, and behilde and seiȝ
That the face of the erthe was dried.

2-3. Variety

James Milroy begins a discussion of Middle English dialectology with this provocative statement: "The most striking fact about Middle English is that it exhibits by far the greatest diversity in written language of any period before or since." ("Middle English Dialectology," in *The Cambridge History of the English Language*, vol. II: 1066–1476, ed. Richard M. Hogg [Cambridge UP: 1992], 156). One of the great accomplishments of the comprehensive research underlying modern approaches to Middle English, in, for example, the *Linguistic Atlas of Late Mediaeval English* (by Angus McIntosh, M.L. Samuels, Michael Benskin [Aberdeen: Aberdeen UP, 1986]) is that such diversity is evident and available for study. It is not the case that Middle English *as a language* necessarily had greater diversity than English at any other time. But because a literary standard for English does not emerge until very late in the ME period, written texts represent linguistic variation in ME to a much greater extent than they did in OE, when late West Saxon had become a literary standard, or in EModE, when the present-day idea of a standard English emerged.

Thus, although we can present in rough outlines the general shape of changes in English during the ME period, when we actually examine a range of ME texts, we can also talk about differences among the dialects of ME. Northern varieties of ME, for example, may be recognized by some of the following features.

Verb
Northern: The third person singular present indicative suffix is *-s/-es*.
Southern: The *-eth* of the third person singular present is retained from OE, often still written as < þ,ð > especially in earlier texts.

Northern: the *-s/-es* of the third person singular present can extend to all other forms in the present, including the first person singular and throughout the plural.
Southern: the suffix in the plural is *-eth*, and in the Midlands, often *-en*.

Pronoun
Northern: the third person plural forms with *th-* in the subject form as well as the possessive and object forms.
Southern: retention of the *h*-forms in the object forms is clear.

Given the differences outlined above, identify the following brief excerpts as representative of Northern or Southern varieties of Middle English. The Northern samples come from the "York Play of the Crucifixion" (J.A. Burrow and Thorlac Turville-Petre, *A Book of Middle English*, 3rd ed. [Blackwell: Malden, MA, 2005]), and the first part of this exercise is based on the treatment of Northern English by Burrow and Turville-Petre. The Southern samples come from Chaucer's *Canterbury Tales*. Remember that the letter <þ>, while gradually replaced with <th>, continued to be used during the ME period. The first is completed for you as an example.

Northern   A.   Al men þat walkis by waye or street,

<small>All men   that   walk   by the way or street,</small>

Takes tente 3e schalle no travayle tyne

<small>Take   heed   you shall   no suffering   fail to see</small>

(You can recognize the Northern feature of the -s suffix for the plural verbs *walkis*
   and *takes*.)

_____ B.   Ille spede þame þat hym spare

<small>Ill   speed   them   that him   spare</small>
<small>May it go badly for them that spare him</small>

_____ C.   The hooly blissful martir for to seke,

<small>The   holy   blissful   martyr   to seek,</small>

That hem hath holpen whan that they were seeke.

<small>That   them   has   helped   when   they   were   sick.</small>

_____ D.   The deeth he feeleth thurgh his herte smyte;

<small>The   death   he feels   through   his heart   smithe</small>

He wepeth, wayleth, crieth, pitously; ...

<small>He   weeps,   wails,   cries,   piteously; ...</small>

_____ E.   þat þai for me may favoure fynde

<small>that they for me   may   favor   find</small>

And fro þe fende þame fende

<small>And   from the fiend   them   defend</small>

2-4. External Events of the ME Period

For each of the following pairs of events, identify which event occurred first, and
explain why, given a reasonable historical narrative and what you have read in the textbook, that one event precedes the other. The first is completed for you as an example.

A. Start of the Hundred Years' War/ Norman Conquest
   The order should be
   1. *Norman Conquest*
   2. *Start of the Hundred Years' War*
   because *the Hundred Years' War is waged in part as a result of the complicated dynastic and political entanglements between England and
   France that occurred when the Duke of Normandy became both the King
   of England and the Duke of Normandy.*

B. Start of the Hundred Years' War / English Peasants' Revolt
The order should be
1.
2.
because

_____

_____

_____

C. Norman Conquest / Marriage of Æþelred and Emma
The order should be
1.
2.
because

_____

_____

_____

D. Norman Conquest / Rule of the Danish kings
The order should be
1.
2.
because

_____

_____

_____

E. English victory at the Battle of Stamford Bridge / Rule of the Danish kings
The order should be
1.
2.
because

_____

_____

_____

F. English Peasants' Revolt / Black Plague
    The order should be
    1.
    2.
    because

    _____

    _____

    _____

PART THREE: ADVANCED EXERCISES

3-1. Early ME

The Anglo-Saxon Chronicle is a very early chronicle in English. The earliest manuscripts date to the 9th century, and the chronicle was maintained and continued into the middle of the twelfth century. For this reason, the Chronicle provides us with rare glimpses into the development of early Middle English from Old English. The following is an excerpt from the Peterborough Chronicle entry for the year 1140. Answer the following questions with reference to this excerpt. The first has been completed for you as an example. (Text of the Anglo-Saxon Chronicle is available through the Labyrinth: Resources for Medieval Studies, http://blogs.commons.georgetown.edu/labyrinth/.)

Þerefter com þe kinges dohter Henries, þe hefde ben emperice in Alamanie (1)

After this   came   the king's   daughter   Henry's,   who had   been   empress   in Germany

After this came King Henry's daughter, who had been empress in Germany

and nu wæs cuntesse in Angou, and com to Lundene;   (2)

and   now was   countess   in Anjou,   and   came   to London;

and te Lundenissce folc hire wolde tæcen, and scæ fleh, and forles þar micel. (3)

And   the London-ish   folk   her   wished   to take,   and   she   fled,   and   abandoned there much

And the people of London wished to capture her, and she fled, and there abandoned much (property).

Þerefter þe biscip of Wincestre, Henri þe kinges brother Stephnes,   (4)

After this   the   bishop   of Winchester,   Henry   the   king's   brother   Stephen's,

After this the bishop of Winchester, Henry, King Stephen's brother,

spac wid Rodbert eorl and wid þemperice, and suor heom athas   (5)

spoke   with   Robert   earl   and   with   the empress,   and   swore   them   oaths

spoke with Earl Robert and with the empress, and swore oaths to them

ðæt he neuere ma mid te king his brother wolde halden,   (6)

that   he   never   more with   the king   his   brother   would   hold,

that he would never ally with his brother the king,

and cursede alle þe men þe mid him heoldon,   (7)

and   cursed   all   the men   who with   him   held,

and cursed all the men who allied with him,

and sæde heom ðat he uuolde iiuen heom up Wincestre,   (8)

and   said   to them   that he   would   give   him   up   Winchester,

and said to them that he would give up Winchester

and dide heom comen þider.   (9)

and   caused them   to come   there.

and caused them to go there.

þa hi þærinne wæren, þa com þe kinges cuen mid al hire strengthe,   (10)

When they therein   were,   then came the king's   queen   with   all her   strength,

and besæt heom, ðat þer wæs inne micel hungær.   (11)

and   beseiged them, so that there was   within great   hunger.

þa hi ne leng ne muhten þolen, þa stalen hi ut and flugen;   (12)

When they no longer not could   endure, then stole   they out and fled;

When they could no longer endure it, they stole out and fled;

and hi wurthen war widuten, and folecheden heom,   (13)

and   they became   aware without,   and   followed   them,

and those outside became aware of this and followed them,

and namen Rodbert eorl of Gloucestre and leeden him to Rouecestre   (14)

and   took   Robert   earl of Gloucester   and   led   him to Rochester

and diden him þare in prisun;   (15)

and   put   him   there in prison;

and te emperice fleh into an minstre.   (16)

and   the empress   fled   into   a   monastery.

A. What are three forms in which this early text shows the definite article?
    þe (line 1)

    _____

    _____

B. The Peterborough Chronicle provides an early example of the replacement of the
    3rd person singular feminine pronoun in line 3. What is the form in this passage?

    _____

    Given your knowledge of OE orthography, how do you think this form might have
    been pronounced?

    _____

C. What is the form of the third person plural subject form of the pronoun through-
    out this excerpt?

    _____

D. In ME and into EModE, the digraph <th> replaces <þ> and <ð>. Obviously both are in use in the Peterborough Chronicle. But the digraph does appear as well. Locate at least two examples in the passage above.

_____

_____

Do you see any pattern which might suggest the path that the replacement might have taken, i.e., where the digraph might have first appeared and where the earlier letters thorn and eth might have persisted longest?

_____

E. What are the regular past tense suffixes for plural verbs in this text?

_____

F. What is the suffix on the infinitive in this text?

_____

G. The passage above uses a form of the inflected genitive that continues to be available in ME and into EModE: *þe kinges dohter Henries* (1.1); *þe kinges brother Stephnes* (1.4). Note that in these phrases, the *-es* inflection on both the word "king" and on the personal names very clearly marks the genitive.

There are two ways we might render these phrases in PDE. One way is with the *of*-genitive: *the daughter of King Henry; the brother of King Stephen.*
But we might also use the inflected genitive: *King Henry's daughter; King Stephen's brother.*

How might we account for the fact that the possessive -s appears on only one of the nouns in the PDE phrases (i.e., not "King's Henry's daughter")?

_____

_____

_____

3-2. Sounds

In exercise 2-1 of this chapter, we considered the addition of a sound in certain contexts. Here, first review the descriptions of the sounds in question in rules 1, 2, and 3, and then answer the question posed below. The first is completed for you as an example. (You may wish to review Chapter Four in the textbook.)

1. [d] is added between [n] and [l] or [r]
2. [p] is added between [m] and [t]
3. [b] is added between [m] and [l] and after final [m]

A. [d] is a *voiced alveolar stop*

  [n] is a _____ _____ _____

  [r] is a _____ _____ _____

B. [p] is a _____ _____ _____

  [m] is a _____ _____ _____

  [t] is a _____ _____ _____

C. [b] is a _____ _____ _____

  [m] is a _____ _____ _____

  [l] is a _____ _____ _____

D. What might account for the introduction of these particular sounds in these contexts?

_____

_____

_____

3-3. Variety

That scholars as well as everyday people heard and recognized regional differences in Middle English is clear from a number of materials. Writing explicitly about language variation, for example, John of Trevisa (1342–1402) claims (expanding on Ranulph Higden's earlier discussion),

> Al þe longage of þe Norþhumbres, and specialych at ʒork, ys so scharp, slyttyng and frotyng, and unschape, þat we Souþeron men may þat longage unneþe undeurstonde.

> All the language of the Northumbrians, and especially at York, is so sharp, piercing and abrasive, and unformed, that we Southern men can hardly understand that language.

(text from Fernand Mossé, *A Handbook of Middle English*, trans. James A. Walker [Baltimore: The Johns Hopkins University Press, 1968, repr. 1991].)

In exercise 2-3 we explored some of the very broad distinctions between Northern and Southern varieties of Middle English. In this exercise we expand that list and consider one instance of *literary* representation of dialect difference.

Chaucer, writing the *Canterbury Tales* at the end of the 14th century, includes one tale in which two characters are identified by the narrator as northerners: "Of o toun were they born, that highte Strother,/ Fer in the north; I kan nat telle where" ("In the same town were they born, called Strother, far in the north; I don't know where"). The text (from the Riverside Chaucer) and interlinear gloss are both taken from Harvard's Geoffrey Chaucer Homepage, http://sites.fas.harvard.edu/~chaucer/teachslf/rvt-par.htm, accessed April 2, 2019.

With the following list in mind, look closely at the speech of these two characters, John and Aleyn.

Verb
Northern: The third person singular present indicative suffix is *-s/-es*.
Southern: The *-eth* of the third person singular present is retained from OE.

Northern: the *-s/-es* of the third person singular present can extend to all other forms in the present, including the first person singular and throughout the plural.
Southern: the suffix in the plural is *-eth*, and in the Midlands, often *-en*.

Northern:
The spread of the *-s* suffix is evident even in the forms of the verb *to be*, which can include *is* as a first person singular form (what Burrow and Turville-Petre call an "extreme Northernism") (*A Book of Middle English*, 3rd ed. [Malden, MA: Blackwell, 2005], 6).

Pronoun
Northern: the third person plural forms with *th-* in the subject form as well as the possessive and object forms.
Southern: retention of the *h*-forms in the object forms is clear.

Phonology/Orthography
Northern: OE /aː/ does not shift to /ɔ/. This /aː/ tends to be spelled with an <a>.
Southern: OE /aː/ becomes /ɔ/ . This /ɔ/ tends to be spelled <o> or <oo>.

"Symond," quod John, "by God, nede has na peer.   (1)
"Symond," said John,   "by God, need knows no law.
Hym   boes   serve hymself that has na swayn,   (2)
Him (it) behoves to serve himself who has no servant,
Or elles he is a fool, as clerkes sayn.   (3)
Or else he is a fool, as clerks say.
Oure manciple, I hope   he wil be deed,   (4)
Our manciple, I expect he will be dead,
Swa werkes ay   the wanges in his heed;   (5)
So   ache   ever the teeth   in his head;

And forthy   is I come, and eek Alayn,   (6)
And therefore am I come, and also Alayn,
To grynde oure corn and carie it ham agayn;   (7)
To grind   our grain and carry it home again;
I pray yow spede us heythen that ye may."   (8)
I pray you speed us hence as fast as you can."

"It shal be doon," quod Symkyn, "by my fay!   (9)
"It shall be done," said Symkyn,   "by my faith!
What wol ye doon whil that it is in hande?"   (10)
What will you do   while   it is at hand?"

"By God, right by the hopur wil I stande,"   (11)
"By God, right by the hopper will I stand,"
Quod John, "and se howgates the corn gas in.   (12)
Said John, "and see how   the grain goes in.

Yet saugh I nevere, by my fader kyn,   (13)
Yet saw   I never,   by my father's kin,
How that the hopur wagges til and fra."   (14)
How   the hopper wags to and fro."

Aleyn answerde, "John, and wiltow swa?   (15)
Aleyn answered, "John, and wilt thou do so?
Thanne wil I be bynethe, by my croun,   (16)
Then   will I be beneath, by my head,
And se how that the mele falles doun   (17)
And see how   the meal falls down

Into the trough; that sal be my disport. (18)
Into the trough; that shall be my sport.
For John, y-faith, I may been of youre sort; (19)
For John, in faith, I may be like you;
I is as ille a millere as ar ye." (20)
I am as poor a miller as are you."

Which of the characteristics of northern varieties of Middle English can you identify in the excerpt above? The first is completed for you as an example.

A. What is the suffix in the present for the third person singular? List four examples.
   -s, in has, line 1

   _____

   _____

   _____

B. What is the suffix in the present for the third person plural? List one example.

   _____

C. What is first person singular form of *to be* in the present? Find two examples of
   that form.

   _____

   _____

D. Find two words you would expect to be spelled with <o> for the /ɔ/ which develops
   in Southern varieties of ME. Note these words are likely to retain the OE <a>
   spelling for the /a/.

   _____

   _____

Neither the character of the Miller nor the narrator in this tale is portrayed as from
the North. How is the language they use different from that of the two Northern
students?

This millere smyled of hir nycetee, (1)
This miller smiled at their foolishness,
   And thoghte, "Al this nys doon but for a wyle. (2)
   And thought, "All this is done only for a trick.
They wene that no man may hem bigyle, (3)
They think that no man can trick them,

But by my thrift, yet shal I blere hir ye, (4)
But by my welfare, yet shall I blear their eyes (fool them),
For al the sleighte in hir philosophye. (5)
Despite all the trickery in their philosophy.

The moore queynte crekes that they make, (6)
The more ingenious tricks that they make,
The moore wol I stele whan I take. (7)
The more will I steal when I take.
In stide of flour yet wol I yeve hem bren. (8)
Instead of flour yet will I give them bran.
The gretteste clerkes been noght wisest men (9)
The greatest clerks are not the wisest men
As whilom to the wolf thus spak the mare. (10)
As once to the wolf thus spoke the mare.
Of al hir art counte I noght a tare." (11)
All their learning I reckon not worth a weed."

Out at the dore he gooth ful pryvely, (12)
Out at the door he goes full stealthily,
Whan that he saugh his tyme, softely. (13)
When he saw his time, quietly.
He looketh up and doun til he hath founde (14)
He looks up and down until he has found
The clerkes hors, ther as it stood ybounde (15)
The clerks' horse, where it stood tied
Bihynde the mille, under a levesel; (16)
Behind the mill, under an arbor;
And to the hors he goth hym faire and wel; (17)
And to the horse he goes gently;
He strepeth of the brydel right anon. (18)
He strips off the bridle right away.

E. What is the third person singular present suffix for the Miller or the narrator?
List three examples.

_____

_____

_____

F. Find two third person plural present forms. What are the likely suffixes for the third person plural present?

_____

_____

G. What are the forms of the third person plural pronoun? List the subject form, the possessive, and the object form.

_____

_____

_____

The representation of dialect differences in this Tale lets us know that speakers of ME heard and were aware of differences in the Englishes used around them.

But, as with representations of dialect differences in literature in PDE, we have to take into consideration the question of how much of the representations we encounter is about the features of the dialect and how much is conveying an *attitude* toward the speakers of that particular variety of the language.

Even in the John of Trevisa passage, for example, consider the ways in which that description of differences is also about an attitude of "we Southern men" towards the dialect spoken in the north. Dialect representation in modern times as well is discussed in Chapter Ten of this workbook.

3-4. Writing in the ME Period

In excercise 1-6 of this chapter, we introduced the cursive used in many manuscripts from the later ME period. Here we will work more closely with an actual ME hand.

Consider the following excerpt from the mid-fourteenth-century manuscript BL Harley MS 2253.

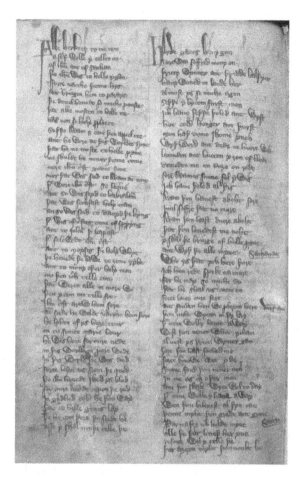

Transliteration and translation of the text:

Alle herkneth to me nou
A strif wolle Y tellen ou
Of Jesu ant of Sathan.
Tho Jesu wes to helle ygan
Forte vacche thenne hys
And bringen hem to parays
The Devel hevede so muche pousté
That alle mosten to helle te.

All listen to me now!
I'll tell you of a contest
Between Jesus and Satan.
When Jesus had gone to hell
To fetch from there his own
And bring them to paradise,
The devil had so much power
That all were made to go to hell.

(Text and translation from *The Complete Harley 2253 Manuscript*, ed. and trans. Susanna Greer Fein, with David Raybin and Jan Ziolkowski, trans. TEAMS Middle English Texts Series [Kalamazoo, MI: Medieval Institute Publications, 2014]. https://d.lib.rochester.edu/teams/publication/fein-harley2253-volume-2. Accessed March 12, 2019.)

A. _____What is the form of the letter <s> in the word "Sathan"? in "parays"? in "pousté"?

B. _____What is the form of the letter <r> in the word "herkeneth"? What is the form of the letter <r> in the word "strif"?

C. _____What is the form of the letter <l> in the words "wolle," "tellen," and "helle"? How are double <l>s formed?

D. _____What is the form of the letter <w> in the word "wolle"?

E. _____What is the form of the letter <y> in the words "y" and "ygan"?

F. _____What is the form of the letter <n> in the words "herkeneth" and "nou"?

G. _____What is the form of the letter <u> in the words "nou" and "on"?

H. _____What is the form of the letter <u> in the words "muche" and "pousté"?

I. _____How are the combinations <th> and <ch> formed ("Sathan," "vacche," "muche")?

J. Which of these letter forms are carried into present-day cursive hands?

_____

K. How might the requirements of cursive (longer segments of text without a pen lift vs. letter-by-letter copying) have an effect on the *content* of what is copied by scribes? Which style might lead to greater care in copying exactly from a source, and which might lead to integration of the scribe's own linguistic habits into the copy?

_____

_____

_____

L. Why?

_____

_____

_____

3-5. Languages in Contact: Literary Culture in the ME Period

The late-thirteenth/early-fourteenth-century BL Harley MS 2253 includes a collection of short poems in English, Anglo-Norman, and Latin. These poems reflect both the fact that literary culture in England was trilingual and also the deep interaction of these languages in that culture. Not only are individual poems written in each of the three languages, but, in a poem like "Dum ludis floribus," the text moves in and out of these languages sometimes in the middle of a line or phrase. (Text and translation from the same source as above.)

Dum ludis floribus velud lacivia,	While you play in flowers as if in lasciviousness
Le Dieu d'Amour moi tient en tiel **angustia,**	The God of Love binds me in such anguish
Merour me tient de duel e **de miseria,**	Holding for me a mirror of sorrow and misery
Si je ne la ay **quam amo super omnia.**	Since I don't have her whom I love above all.

. . .

Scripsi hec carmina in tabulis.	I've written these songs on a tablet
Mon ostel est enmi la vile de Paris.	My lodging's amid the city of Paris
May Y sugge namore, so wel me is;	I may say not more, as seems best;
Yef Hi deye for love of hire, duel hit ys!	Should I die for love of her, sad it is!

These are the first and last stanzas of the poem. The phrases in bold are in Latin, in regular font are in Anglo-Norman, and in italics are in Middle English.

A. What does the pattern of shifts between Anglo-Norman and Latin suggest to you about the function of those languages in the literary culture?

_____

_____

_____

B. Some scholars have suggested that the narrator of this poem is a student. How might the movement between languages here reflect the intellectual life of an English *student* in the Middle English period?

_____

_____

_____

C. What is the force of the shift to Middle English for the final two lines? These are the only two lines in Middle English in the entire poem.

_____

_____

_____

D. Note that the ME word "duel" (meaning "sad") occurs in the last line of the poem. You may have noticed that it also occurs in the third line of the poem, but in Anglo-Norman! There "duel" is the noun translated as "sorrow." The ME word is borrowed, not surprisingly, from Old French. But the Old French word develops from Latin. Does knowledge of that layering influence your interpretation of the poem?

_____

_____

_____

Notes

Notes

Chapter Nine

PART ONE: BEGINNING EXERCISES

1-1. Review for the Great Vowel Shift (GVS)

In order to make sense of the systematic repositioning of long vowels that occurred during the EModE period, one first has to have a firm grasp of the IPA symbols for the vowels in question. For many students, what may seem like confusion about the Great Vowel Shift is actually confusion about the IPA. For most speakers of PDE, it is the vowel symbols that are the most difficult symbols to integrate into an understanding of the IPA; this is precisely because of the changes brought about in the course of the Great Vowel Shift! So our first exercise here will be a review of the IPA symbols, the sounds they represent, and their placement in the schematic "vowel trapezoid" we have used to visualize their places of articulation. (You should review the relevant material in Chapter Four of the textbook.)

For each of the words in the following list, a very broad phonetic transcription is provided. First pronounce the vowel, and then provide the PDE spelling of the word. (Note that we use here very broad transcription for the vowels, we are not representing the off-glides for [e] and [o] that would certainly be part of a more precise representation, and there may be more than one possible representation of a particular vowel in PDE orthography!) The first is completed for you as an example.

IPA   PDE spelling
A. [si]   *see* or *sea*
B. [wi]   _____ or _____
C. [ɹot]   _____ or _____
D. [mɛt]   _____

E. [ɑi] _____ or _____ or _____

F. [flɑuɹ] _____ or _____

G. [tɑun] _____

H. [et] _____ or _____

I. [æt] _____

J. [fet] _____

K. [fit] _____ or _____

L. [mod] _____ or _____

M. [mud] _____ or _____

N. [sun] _____

O. [so] _____ or _____ or _____

P. [tɒt] _____

Q. [tæp] _____

R. [tep] _____

S. [bɑks] _____

T. [ɑks] _____

It is a little harder to go in the other direction, from a PDE spelling or two to the IPA, so here is our next review. The first is completed for you as an example.

PDE spelling	IPA (for the vowel only, and broadly)
U. tea, tee, or ti	[i]
V. main or mane	_____
W. due or do	_____
X. tow or toe	_____
Y. hi, hie, or high	_____
Z. hour or our	_____
AA. back	_____
BB. bother	_____
CC. aw (as in "Aw shucks!")	_____
DD. scene or seen	_____

Finally, work on disambiguating IPA and PDE spelling further as you identify which word in PDE spelling is pronounced with the vowel provided in IPA. The first is completed for you as an example.

EE.   [ɛ]   a. seat
           b. set   X

FF.   [e]   a. cape
           b. cap

GG.   [ɑ]   a. pope
           b. Pa

HH.   [o]   a. boon
           b. bone

II.   [i]   a. wheat
           b. wit

JJ.   [u]   a. toot
           b. taught

KK.   [ɑi] a. bite
           b. bait

LL.   [ɑu] a. clod
           b. cloud

MM.   [æ]   a. Keats
           b. cats

NN.   [i]   a. we
           b. why

OO.   Finally, fill in the following chart mapping, in very broad phonetic terms
      and using IPA symbols, of the GVS. You may wish to review the presentation
      in Chapter Nine before you do so. The first is completed for you as an example.

Pre-GVS		Post-GVS
i	>	ɑi
e	>	___
ɛ	>	___
æ	>	___

u	>	_____
o	>	_____
ɑ	>	_____
ɔ	>	_____

1-2. Thou and You

As discussed in Chapter Nine of the textbook, although the distinction is already clearly evidenced in ME, in EModE, the distinction between the *thou* forms and the *you* forms is not only about number but also about politeness. Consider the following passage from Malory's late 15th-century *Morte Darthur*. (Text is from Sir Thomas Malory, *Le Morte Darthur: The Winchester Manuscript*, edited by Helen Cooper [Oxford: Oxford UP, 2008], 485–86.) In this passage, Sir Gawain is enraged because Sir Lancelot has accidentally killed his kinsmen. Lancelot is ultimately careful and apologetic. Pay attention to the use of the *thou* and *you* forms.

1. "Fie on thee, false recrayed knight!" said Sir Gawain, "for I let thee wit, my lord, my uncle King Arthur, shall have his queen and thee both, maugre thy visage, and slay you both and save you whether it please him."
2. "It may well be," said Sir Lancelot. "But wit thou well, my lord Sir Gawain, and me list to come out of this castle, ye should win me and the queen more harder than ever ye won a strong battle."
3. "Now fie on thy proud words!" said Sir Gawain. "As for my lady the Queen, wit thou well I will never say her shame. But thou false and recrayed knight," said Sir Gawain, "what cause hadst thou to slay my good brother Sir Gareth, that loved thee more than me and all my kin? ..."
4. "That me repents," said Sir Lancelot, "for well I understand it booteth me not to seek no accord while ye, Sir Gawain, are so mischievously set. And if ye were not, I would not doubt to have the good grace of my lord King Arthur."

A. Which character uses the *thou* forms more frequently?

_____

B. What does the use of the *thou* forms accomplish for that character? Why might he choose them in this context?

_____

_____

C. Which character uses the *you* forms more frequently?

_____

D. What does the use of the *you* forms accomplish for that character? Why might he choose them in this context?

_____

_____

E. Why does Gawain use the *you* forms in section 1? What does the difference between the *thou* and the *you* forms signify in this section?

_____

_____

F. Although Lancelot tends to use the *you* forms to refer to Gawain, he does use *thou* once in section 2. What might explain this use of *thou* rather than *ye* here?

_____

_____

1-3. Morphology

Throughout the history of English, strong verbs have become weak. In an appendix to his 1772 *Rudiments of Grammar*, Joseph Priestly provides a list of troublesome verbs, "verbs irregularly inflected" that reflect this tendency, excerpted below (Joseph Priestly, *The Rudiments of English Grammar: Adapted to the Use of Schools*, 3rd ed. [London: J. and F. Rivington, 1772], 47–52). Which of the verbs he identifies are still "troublesome" and which have become weak in PDE? Which are clearly still in motion?

arise	arose	arisen		meet	met	met
bid	bade	bidden		ride	rode	ridden
bind	bound	bound		set	set	set
blow	blew	blown		shine	shone	shone
break	brake	broken, broke		shoe	shod	shod
burst	burst	burst, bursten		slay	slew	slain
cling	clung	clung		smite	smote	smitten
dare	durst	dared		spit	spat	spitted
die	died	dead		strive	strove	striven
draw	drew	drawn		swing	swung	swung
drive	drove	drove		thrive	throve	thriven
fling	flung	flung		work	wrought	wrought
freeze	froze	frozen		wring	wrung	wrung
hurt	hurt	hurt				

(continued)

lay	laid	laid, lain
lead	led	led
lie	lay	lain

A. verbs which have become weak in PDE

_____

_____

B. verbs for which both past tenses are acceptable (answers may vary!)

_____

_____

_____

_____

1-4. Morphology and Syntax

In his *Short Introduction to English Grammar*, Robert Lowth identifies the simple present and past tense forms of verbs, but he also explains, "But to express the time of the verb the English uses also the assistance of other verbs, called therefore Auxiliaries, or Helpers; *do, be, have, shall, will*; as 'I *do* love, I *did* love; I *am* loved, I *was* loved; I *have* loved, I *have been* loved; I *shall*, or *will*, love, or *be* loved'" (Robert Lowth, *A Short Introduction to English Grammar: With Critical Notes* [Philadelphia: R. Aiken, 1799], 33. Internet Archive. https://archive.org/details/shortintroductio00lowtrich/page/n3. Accessed March 15, 2019.)

Review the synopsis of the verb provided in Chapters Two and Nine. Identify the constructions below as present, past, or future, as active or passive, and as progressive, perfect, or perfect-progressive. The first is completed for you as an example.

A. I am loved   present passive

B. I was loved   _____

C. I have loved   _____

D. I have been loved   _____

E. I shall/will love   _____

F. I shall/will be loved   _____

The appearance of *do love* in Lowth's list perhaps reflects the expansion in the use of the *do* as an auxiliary during the EModE period more than what is strictly necessary for expressing solely "the time of the verb."

Increasingly in EModE, as in PDE, however, *do* is required as an auxiliary in a number of contexts, as illustrated below:

G. Make the sentence "I love" negative.

_____

H. Make the sentence "I love" a yes or no question.

_____

I. Ask the speaker a direct question about whom or what s/he loves.

_____

1-5. Lexicon

The EModE period witnesses an unprecedented expansion of the lexicon. A large number of the new words are "inkhorn terms": intentional, learned borrowings, often replacing or supplementing extant words which may not have seemed technical or weighty enough to scholars and others producing texts during this period. The following exercise provides you with a short list of possible Latin words to draw from. From that list, create at least two new words that do not already exist in English. (Such new forms are known as neologisms.) For example, you might create *formical* to mean "ant-like" or *claudic* to mean "closed in." Afterwards, check the *Oxford English Dictionary* to find out whether the words you created have actually occurred in English at some time or another.

English	Latin	English	Latin
about	circa	close (v)	claudo
above	super	dawn	aurora
abstain	(v) abstineo, abstinere	dead	mortuus
after	post	donkey	asinus
air	aether	duty	officium
alien	alienus	face	vultus
ant	formica	finger	digitus
apple	malum	itch (v)	prurio
art	ars	lettuce	lactuca
baboon	simia	moon	luna
bare	nudus	myth	fabula
bat	vespertilio	near	prope
beer	fermentum	over	super

before	ante	often	saepe
beneath	sub		
body	corpus, corporis		
brain	cerebrum		
cave	spelunca		
chicken	pullus		
chief	princeps		

A. _____, _____

PART TWO: INTERMEDIATE EXERCISES

2-1. Orthography and Phonology

A point made in the textbook as well as earler in this chapter, and in last chapter of the workbook is that modern English spelling often reflects much older pronunciation of the language. The effect is that the orthography of English is often described as chaotic or needlessly complex. However, even in modern times, it has changed sometimes in ways that may have been intended to disambiguate some words. (And sometimes it has been changed to identify the location of the English in question, for example American English *color* and British English *colour*.)

One orthographic convention that developed in the Early Modern period was the representation of /ɛ:/ with <ea>. Another was the representation of /ɔ:/ with <oa>.

In ME, the /ɛ:/ which developed from OE /æ: / tended to be spelled with <e> or <ee>. The word meaning *sea* in ME would have been spelled <se> or <see>. In ME, the /ɔ:/ which developed from OE /a:/ tended to be spelled with <o> or <oo>. The word meaning *moan* in ME would have been spelled <mone> or <moon>. Note that one result of these changes is that a new set of homophones or homographs develops (*see* as part of the verb *to see*, *see* as the ocean; *moon* or *mone* as the celestial body, *mone* or *moon* as "to lament"). The introduction of the <ea> and <oa> spellings allows for some disambiguation of those words as they appear in writing.

But not all of the words with these new spellings shifted during the GVS. Possible PDE pronunciations of <ea> and <oa> words reflect the uneven shifting of those sounds, including the fact that in some words the earlier vowels may not have shifted much at all.

Provide the IPA equivalent of the PDE vowel for the following words and indicate whether or not the PDE pronunciation reflects the sound changes of the GVS. Note that responses may vary depending on the variety of English you speak! The first is completed for you as an example.

	PDE vowel	shows the GVS or not fully or not at all?
A. clean	[i]	*yes*
B. steak	_____	_____
C. pea	_____	_____
D. break	_____	_____

E. great   _____   _____

F. road   _____   _____

G. loan   _____   _____

H. broad   _____   _____

I. foam   _____   _____

2-2. The Perfect with *have* and *be*

In ME, the perfect was formed with either *have* or *be* as the auxiliary with the past participle. The rule for the formation of the perfect was that *have* was used with transitive verbs and *be* was used with intransitive verbs, particularly those denoting motion.

Although increasingly in the EModE period *have* develops into the only auxiliary for most verbs, in a number of phrases the *be* auxiliary is retained for certain verbs and in certain contexts.

The King James Bible (KJB), as we know, tended to be quite conservative in some of its language. It also tended toward formulaic language, including grammar. In the KJB, *be* + *come* occurs at least 333 times, and *be* + *gone* occurs at least 111 times.

Similar counts might be made of *be*+past participle perfects in other kinds of texts across the EModE period, however. As late as the mid 19th century, and even later, examples of *be* + come are rather easy to find, and *be* + go still exists in English as in *Carter is already gone.*

A. Why do you think that *come* and *go* might have retained their *be* auxiliaries longer than other verbs did?

_____

_____

_____

2-3. The Table Alphabeticall

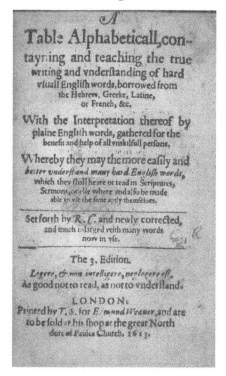

This image of the title page for Robert Cawdry's *Table Alphabetical* provides a great deal of insight into the motivations for prescription as well as general attitudes towards the language. The title page for the 1604 edition was almost identical to this one, except that its "interpretation by plaine English words" was "gathered for the benefit and helpe of Ladies, Gentlewomen, or any other unskilfull persons." The full text of the 1604 edition follows.

A Table Alphabeticall, conteyning and teaching the true writing, and vnderstanding of hard usuall English words, borrowed from the Hebrew, Greeke, Latine, or French. &c.

With the interpretation thereof by plaine English words, gathered for the benefit and helpe of Ladies, Gentlewomen, or any other unskilfull persons.

Whereby they may the more easilie and better understand many hard English words, which they shall heare or read in Scriptures, Sermons, or elsewhere, and also be made able to use the same aptly themselves.

Legere, et non intelligere, neglegere est.
As good not read, as not to understand.

A. What does the way in which this text presents itself to its intended readers suggest about some effects of the standardization of spelling?

_____

_____

B. Who are the people who make up the target audience for this list of hard words?

_____

_____

C. What does the fact that this book directs itself to these people in particular suggest?

_____

_____

D. Why does the text suggest they will want to use this list?

_____

_____

E. Why is the Latin motto translated into English?

_____

_____

F. What is the difference between understanding and using a word "aptly"?

_____

_____

G. Why is the table presented in alphabetical order?

_____

_____

PART THREE: ADVANCED EXERCISES

3-1. Orthography and Phonology

Although we tend to consider starting points somewhere in late ME and tentative stopping points in the early part of Modern English, the Great Vowel Shift happened, like all sound changes, gradually and not in all varieties at once. In fact, it may not even be sensible to think of it as "complete." Since we do not have sound recordings for the EModE period, and since spelling is increasingly fixed during the period, we are somewhat limited in the means we have for tracking the shifts. The literary use of end rhyme, which becomes a feature of verse in English in the ME period and continues throughout the EModE period, can provide some insight into the place of certain vowels as the shift progresses.

Consider each of the following rhymes. Assuming that the end sounds in the rhymes were close enough at the time the text was written, and in the variety of English in which it was written, that they can be considered rhymes and not intentional literary violations of the convention, what information about the vowel sounds does the rhyme provide?

As an often-quoted example, Alexander Pope, in the early 18th century, could rhyme "obey" with "tea" in the following lines from "Rape of the Lock":

> Here Thou, Great Anna! Whom three Realms **obey**,
> Dost sometimes Counsel take—and sometimes **Tea**

If we accept that the rhyme actually worked in Pope's day, either "tea" or "obey" had a significantly different vowel at that time than it does in most English varieties today. And given that we know that both /ɛ/ and /e/ shifted during the GVS to /i/; and that /ɛ/ likely moved through /e/ as it raised to /i/, we might conclude that the vowel in "tea" did not shift in all varieties to /i/, or that it was in the process of shifting at the time that Pope was writing.

For this exercise, first write the bolded vowel of the rhymed words in IPA as you would pronounce them in PDE. Then write a sentence or two about what their rhyme in the Early Modern period suggests about the effects of the Great Vowel Shift on those words at that time. The first part of the first item is completed for you as an example.

A. Edmund Spencer, *The Faerie Queene* (1596)

	your vowel in IPA
But he the knight, whose semblaunt he did **beare**,	___[ɛ]_____

The true Saint George was wandred far away,
Still flying from his thoughts and gealous **feare**;   ___[i]_____
Will was his guide, and griefe led him astray
(Book I, Canto II, stanza 12)

The Sarazin was stougt, and wondrous strong,
And heaped blowes like yron hammers **great**:   _____
For after bloud and vengeance he did long.
The knight was fiers, and full of youthly **heat**:   _____
And doubled strokes, like dreaded thunders **threat**:   _____
For all for prayse and honour he did fight.
Both stricken strike, and beaten both do **beat**...   _____
  (Book I, Canto V, stanza 7)

_____

_____

_____

Edmund Spencer, *The Faerie Queene*, edited by Thomas P. Roche Jr. with C. Patrick O'Donnell Jr. (New Haven: Yale University Press, 1981).

B. William Shakespeare, Sonnets (1609)

So all their praises are but **prophecies**   _____
Of this our time, all you prefiguring.
And for they looked but with divining **eyes**   _____
They had not skill enough your worth to sing ...
Sonnet 106

For there can live no hatred in thine **eye**   _____
Therefore in that I cannot know thy change.
In many's looks, the false heart's **history**   _____
Is writ in moods and frowns and wrinkles strange ...
Sonnet 93

Is it thy spirit that thou sends from thee
So far from home into my deeds to **pry**,   _____
To find out shames and idle hours in me,
The scope and tenor of thy **jealousy**?   _____
Sonnet 61

When I perceive that men as plants increase
Cheered and checked ev'n by the selfsame **sky**,   _____
Vaunt in their youthful sap, at height decrease,
And wear their brave state out of **memory**;   _____
Sonnet 15

_____

_____

_____

William Shakespeare, *Shakespeare's Sonnets*, edited by Stephen Booth (New Haven: Yale University Press, 1977).

C. John Donne (1633)

His drinke was counterfeit, as was his **meat**;   _____
For, eyes which rowle towards all, weep not, but **sweat**.   _____
"Love's Diet"

He which doth not, his error is as **great**,   _____
As who by Clyster gave the Stomack **meat**.   _____
"Elegie XVIII, Loves Progress"

_____

_____

_____

John Donne, *John Donne Poetry and Prose*, edited by Frank J. Warnke (New York: Modern Library, 1967).

D. William Blake's famous poem "The Tyger" opens and ends with the following lines:

Tyger Tyger burning bright,
In the forests of the night:
What immortal hand or eye,
Dare frame thy fearful symmetry?

Blake published this poem at the end of the 18th century.

The rhyme "eye/symmetry" has occasioned considerable literary commentary around the question of whether the lines actually rhyme, given that the literal question they pose is about "fearful symmetry" and order in divine creation. If they do not actually rhyme, the discord in the final lines is surely significant to a literary interpretation. But given what you know about the Great Vowel Shift, and the similar rhymes you have seen above, how, from the perspective of a scholar of the history of the English language, might you add nuance to the interpretation of these lines?

_____

_____

_____

3-2. Lexicon

Although we focus on the enormous number of borrowings into English during the EModE period from Classical languages, it is important to remember that the EModE period is also, to put it in seemingly neutral terms, "The Age of Exploration." The integration of some words borrowed during this period into English is in some cases so complete that it may be difficult to recognize these words as borrowed in the present day. (And see exercise 2-4 in Chapter Three.)

Match the following words with the language from which they are borrowed and the date of their earliest citation in English. You may need to consult a dictionary with etymological information, like the *OED*.

A. _____ lilac   G. _____ serendipity

B. _____ persimmon   H. _____ jasmine

C. _____ punch (the drink)   I. _____ ketchup

D. _____ cola (the tree)   J. _____ pyjama, pajama

E. _____ barbeque   K. _____ bangle

F. _____ cummerbund   L. _____ cushy

1. from Hindi, 1787
2. from French, from Persian, 1658
3. from Algonquian, 1612
4. partly from Urdu, partly from Persian, 1887
5. from Sanskrit, 1500
6. from West African languages, 1795

7. from Spanish from Haiti; also from French from the Indians of Guyana, 1697
8. from a former name for Sri Lanka, 1754
9. from Urdu and Persian, 1616
10. from Chinese, 1682
11. multiple forms in European languages, all of which derive from Arabic, 1578
12. from Urdu and Persian, 1801

3-3. Clitics

In Chapter Nine of the textbook we discuss the possible reanalysis of the inflected genitive as a clitic, and the subsequent expansion of that clitic into *his*, and extension to *her* and *their*.

In this exercise we examine how clitics work in a little more detail than was possible in the chapter in the textbook.

In languages like English with strong stress on lexical words, more weakly stressed grammatical words, like auxiliary verbs or negators, can become significantly reduced in speech. *The rabbits will eat the grass*, for example, can become *The rabbits'll eat the grass*.

When this kind of reduction occurs, the reduced form, *'ll*, will attach to words it occurs close to. One feature of clitics is that while they may, as in the case of *'ll*, seem to be dependent on a particular class of word (here a noun, and the subject of the verb *will*), the clitic will attach to a word of whatever class is next to it. So you can say, for example, *The rabbit you saw yesterday'll eat the grass*, or *The rabbit that John bought'll eat the grass*.

Furthermore, given the set of clitics in English, we understand a clitic as most often expandable: *'ll* can be expanded to *will* without changing the literal meaning of the sentence at all.

So, features of clitics, at least many of them in English, include:
    a. They begin as grammatical or function words.
    b. They are reduced forms of those grammatical words.
    c. They attach to a word next to them.
    d. The do not necessarily attach only to words of one class.
    e. They can be expanded to their fuller form.

With reference to the above list of features of clitics, identify the following as either clitics or simply abbreviated words. The first is completed for you as an example.

A. 's, as in *That book's marvelous—I could read it ten more times.*
   Shows feature (a.)?
   Yes, the word "is," the copula, is a grammatical word

   Shows feature (b.)?
   _____

   Shows feature (c.)?
   _____

   Shows feature (d.)?
   _____

   Shows feature (e.)?
   _____

B. 're, as in *When e're you make a promise, deliver well its importance.*
   Shows feature (a.)?
   _____

   Shows feature (b.)?
   _____

   Shows feature (c.)?
   _____

   Shows feature (d.)?
   _____

   Shows feature (e.)?
   _____

C. 'er, as in *O'er the hills and through the woods to Grandmother's house we go.*
   Shows feature (a.)?
   _____

   Shows feature (b.)?
   _____

Shows feature (c.)?

_____

Shows feature (d.)?

_____

Shows feature (e.)?

_____

D. *'ve* as in *The students've outdone themselves this time.*
Shows feature (a.)?

_____

Shows feature (b.)?

_____

Shows feature (c.)?

_____

Shows feature (d.)?

_____

Shows feature (e.)?

_____

Remember that the regular suffix for the possessive forms of almost all nouns was *-s*, or *-es*.

One possible explanation for the development of the *his*-genitive (see Chapter Nine in the textbook) is that speakers heard the possessive inflection *-es* on certain words, or even saw, in writing, the representation of that inflection as *'s*, and understood it as a **different** structure, as a clitic rather than the inflection for the possessive.

E. If a speaker understood the *-es* or *-s* on a word like *Augustuses*, as in *Augustuses heart*, as a clitic, not an inflection, which of the features of the clitic listed above might explain the appearance of *Augustus his heart*?

_____

3-4. Prescription and Usage

We have discussed some of the motivations and the methods for justifying grammatical prescriptions during the EModE period in Chapter Nine of the textbook. In this exercise, we ask you to think a little more about what might underlie the persistence of the prescribed forms or constructions.

A. *It is I* is supposed to be more correct than *It's me*. Why does *It's me* persist? What makes *It's me* work for speakers of English?

_____

_____

B. Similarly, *She is older than I* is supposed to be more correct than *She is older than me*. Why will most of us say *She is older than me*?

_____

_____

C. Why are split infinitives so common? Why would most of us rather say *to boldly go* than *to go boldly*?

_____

_____

D. Why, when a singular pronoun form is supposed to be more correct, do we use *their* to refer to a singular referent, as in *Each student should bring their book to class*?

_____

_____

It is not the case that prescription is simply imposed by grammarians and simply resisted by speakers on account of "natural" tendencies in the language. One phenomenon that makes very clear the power of prescription is hypercorrection, in which speakers come to change a form in a particular context because of the force of a prescription elsewhere.

For example, the form of the first person singular pronoun in the phrase *between you and I* would historically have been *me*, because *me* is the object form of the pronoun, and *me* is the object of the preposition *between*.

E. Why is the phrase *between you and I* now so pervasive? What is the prescription that this construction is a likely response to?

_____

3-5. The King James Bible and EModE

First a few review questions.

A. What is increasingly the expected 3rd person singular present suffix on the verb in EModE? _____

B. What has the distinction between the *thou* and the *you* forms of the second person pronoun come to mark (more than number)? _____

C. What will happen to the second person singular present suffix on the verb in the course of EModE? _____

PSAL. XXIII.

Dauids confidence in Gods grace.

¶ A Psalme of Dauid.

The LORD is * my shep-
heard, I shall not want.

2 He maketh me to lie
downe in † greene pa-
stures: he leadeth mee beside the † still waters.

3 He restoreth my soule: he leadeth
me in the pathes of righteousnes, for
his names sake.

4 Yea though I walke through the
valley of the shadowe of death,* I will
feare no euill: for thou art with me, thy
rod and thy staffe, they comfort me.

5 Thou preparest a table before me,
in the presence of mine enemies : thou
† anointest my head with oyle, my cuppe
runneth ouer.

6 Surely goodnes and mercie shall
followe me all the daies of my life : and
I will dwell in the house of the LORD
for euer.

Consider the text of the 23rd Psalm as it appears in the 1611 edition of the King James Bible.

1. [A Psalme of Dauid.] The Lord is my shepheard, I shall not want.
2. He maketh me to lie downe in greene pastures: he leadeth mee beside the still waters.
3. He restoreth my soule: he leadeth me in the pathes of righteousness, for his names sake.
4. Yea though I walke through the valley of the shadowe of death, I will feare no euill: for thou art with me, thy rod and thy staffe, they comfort me.
5. Thou preparest a table before me, in the presence of mine enemies: thou anointest my head with oyle, my cuppe runneth o[v]er.
6. Surely goodness and mercie shall followe me all the daies of my life: and I will dwell in the house of the lord for euer.

D. What is consistently the third person singular present suffix on the verb in this passage? _____

E. Which pronoun form is used to refer to God? _____

F. What is the second person singular present suffix on the verb in this passage? _____

G. What might explain the tension between the forms identified here and what we have discussed as the general tendencies of the language during the EModE period? That is, given that there were other forms available, why might the composers of the King James Bible have selected these forms?

_____

_____

_____

_____

(Image and text from The King James Bible Online, https://www.kingjamesbible-online.org/Psalms-Chapter-23_Original-1611-KJV/ Accessed March 15, 2019.)

3-6. Syntax

In Chapter Seven we described the syntax of Old English as largely paratactic and noted that strategies for subordination developed as the English became more widely used in literate contexts. The EModE period provides vivid evidence of the development of those strategies.

Consider the following *long* sentence which makes up these famous opening lines to John Milton's epic 17th-century poem, *Paradise Lost*:

Of Man's First Disobedience, and the Fruit
Of that Forbidden Tree, whose mortal taste
Brought Death into the World, and all our woe,
With loss of Eden, till one greater Man
Restore us, and regain the blissful Seat,
Sing Heav'nly Muse, that on the secret top
Of Oreb, or of Sinae, didst inspire
That Shepherd, who first taught the chosen Seed,
In the Beginning how the Heav'ns and Earth
Rose out of Chaos: Or if Sion Hill
Delight thee more, and Siloa's Brook that flow'd

Fast by the Oracle of God; I thence
Invoke thy aid to my advent'rous Song,
That with no middle flight intends to soar
Above th'Aonian Mount, while it pursues
Things unattempted yet in Prose or Rhyme.

(John Milton, *Paradise Lost*. In Merritt Y. Hughes, ed. *John Milton: Complete Poems and Major Prose* [Indianapolis: Bobbs-Merrill Educational Publishing, 1957], 211.)

First, for each of the finite verbs in this passage, provide their subjects and objects. Note that some of these subjects may be relative pronouns like *that* or *who*.

For example, the first finite verb is *brought*, in line 3. The subject of that verb is *taste* and it has two direct objects, *death* and *woe*

taste	**brought**	*death*	and	*woe*
Subject		Direct Object		Direct Object

A. _____ **restore** _____

    Subject   Direct Object

B. _____ **regain** _____

    Subject   Direct Object

C. **sing**

D. _____ **didst inspire** _____

    Subject   Direct Object

E. _____ **taught** _____ _____

    Subject   Indirect Object   Direct Object (an entire clause!)

F. _____ and _____ **rose**

    Subject   Subject

G. _____ and _____ **delight** _____

    Subject   Subject   Direct Object

H. _____ **flow'd**

    Subject

I. _____ **invoke** _____

    Subject   Direct Object

J. _____ **intends**
      Subject

K. _____ **pursues** _____
      Subject   Direct Object

As you know from Chapter Two, relative clauses are often called "adjective clauses" because they modify nouns. Identify the *five* relative clauses in this sentence and the noun that each one modifies.

L. _____

    modifies _____

M. _____

    modifies _____

N. _____

    modifies _____

O. _____

    modifies _____

P. _____

    modifies _____

Other strategies for subordination in this sentence include adverb clauses (introduced with the subordinate conjunctions *till* and *while*) and a noun clause (a clause derived from a *Wh-* question, beginning with *how*).

An additional complication in this sentence is the fact that its two independent clauses are joined by a semicolon (at line 12).

If we were to strip this sentence to its most basic elements, the finite verb of the first independent clause, and the subject, verb, and direct object of the second independent clause, what would that very stripped-down sentence look like? In order to find these forms, you may need to cross out the prepositional phrases, relative clauses, and other subordinate clauses in the sentence!

Q. _____; _____ _____ _____
     verb   Subject   verb   Direct Object

R. What does Milton accomplish by presenting the matter of this poem in this opening sentence with such (almost unreadably!) complex syntax?

_____

_____

_____

_____

_____

_____

3-7. Lexicon

In section 1-5 you were asked to generate two new "inkhorn terms." Here we ask you to return to those terms and provide an argument for why these words are "necessary," or why they are "better" words than a compound you might have made from native English elements. Try to be as specific as possible. You might say, for example, "They just sound better." But if so, try to articulate why they sound "better."

A. _____

_____

_____

_____

Notes

Chapter Ten

1-1. Circles of English

As we will see in a later exercise, Kachru's model of World Englishes divided into inner, outer, and expanding circles may not always capture some of the nuances concerning the many different ways in which English is regarded, spoken, written, and learned around the globe. Nevertheless, the model is a reasonable starting point for us to begin understanding the dynamics of English as it is used in different countries. Based on the description of the use of English below, do speakers fall into Kachru's inner, outer, or expanding circle? (Note that the term *de jure* official language means that the language is official by law, whereas *de facto* official language means that the language is "official" by practice or common usage.)

Ghana

In Ghana's first constitution in 1957, English had the status of a de facto official language as it required members of parliament be able to use English. In later versions of the constitution, English is not mentioned and preference is shown toward the use of indigenous languages. Magnus Huber writes, "This reflects the general feeling among Ghanaians that English is a borrowed, foreign language and a residue of colonialism" (847) (Magnus Huber, "Ghanaian English: Phonology," in *A Handbook of Varieties of English: Phonology* [Berlin: Mouton de Gruyter, 2004], 842–65).

A. *Outer circle: English is not a native language but was used as a language of government*

New Zealand
In c. 1000 CE, Polynesian travelers settled on New Zealand; the language they spoke was Maori. Waves of immigration and settlement by British and Australians throughout the 19th century have resulted in a majority of English speakers since c. 1850. Today, only about 3.7% of the population are conversant in Maori, while 96.1% speak English. The official business of government, courts, and schools is almost exclusively in English.

B. _____

Russia
Russia abounds in languages. While only Russian is recognized at the federal level, 25 or so other languages are official within the various republics that make up the Russian Confederation. English is taught and learned as a foreign language, albeit an immensely popular one. In one study carried out in 2014, 80% of those who claimed to be able to speak a foreign language indicated that the language they could speak was English.

C. _____

Japan
Japanese, spoken by nearly all of the population of Japan, is the de facto official language of Japan. English classes are compulsory starting from the 5th grade, and by the time a Japanese student has graduated from high school, he/she will have studied English for 8 years. However, unlike some other countries in which English instruction is integral throughout the school curriculum, most Japanese report their ability to use English, especially in speaking, to be quite low. For this reason, private teaching and tutoring of English in Japan has become a lucrative industry.

D. _____

Canada
Home to more than 90 languages, both Indigenous and immigrant, Canada lists both English and French as its official languages. 56.9% of the population report English as their mother tongue, while 85.6% claim working knowledge of the language, compared to 21.3% and 30.1% respectively for French. The relationship between English and French speakers has not always been an easy one, and understandably French speakers have resisted the encroachment of English into traditional French-speaking communities. At various times, French-speaking areas of Canada have even sought to secede and become independent.

E. _____

Vanuatu

Vanuatu has a complex colonial history in that it was colonially administered by both Britain and France, with the result that both the English and French languages were firmly established in government, business, and schools. After independence, an English-based pidgin, Bislama, was established as the official language, along-side English and French. While Bislama is the most widely spoken language used for day-to-day interaction, English continues in use in many sectors of government and in education.

F. _____

1-2. Pidgins and Creoles: Trinidadian and Tobagonian Creole

This exercise is based on Winford James and Valerie Youssef's chapter, "The Creoles of Trinidad and Tobago: Morphology and Syntax," in *A Handbook of Varieties of English: Morphology and Syntax* (Berlin: Mouton de Gryuter, 2004), 454–81.

The English-lexified creoles spoken on the two islands that make up the nation Trinidad and Tobago are largely overlapping, particularly in their mesolectal varieties.[1] Commonly in creoles, particularly in basilectal varieties, pronouns show no changes for case. Thus, the way one says "I" is "mi" and the way one says "me" is "mi."[2] However, as we move into mesolectal varieties, some creoles will show case in pronouns, although with patterns that differ from those of the lexifier language, English. The pronouns for Trinidadian and Tobagonian are as follows:

	Subject Forms			Object Forms	
	singular	plural		singular	plural
1st	a	wi	1st	mi	wi
2nd	yu		2nd	yu	
3rd m.	hi	de	3rd m.	im	dem
f.	shi	de	f.	shi	dem
n.	i	de	n.	it	dem

---

1 You will recall from the textbook that it is common to refer to various levels of a creole as basilectal, mesolectal, and acrolectal. Basilectal is the purest creole form and acrolectal is the variety of the creole most like the lexifier language. Mesolectal varieties are somewhere between the basilectal and acrolectal forms.

2 It is customary to spell creoles phonetically and not to over-impose English spelling.

Based on the forms given above, provide the pronoun for the simple sentences given. The first is completed for you as an example.

A. *hi luv³ wi*   'He loves us.'

B. _____ see_____   'She sees him.'

C. _____ hav _____   'We have it.'

D. _____ keri _____   'It takes him.'

E. _____ laik _____   'You like them.'

F. _____ kos _____   'She curses her.'

G. _____ iit _____   'I eat it.'

H. _____ beliiv _____   'They believe me.'

I. _____ tiich _____   'We teach them.'

J. _____ bai _____   'You buy it.'

1-3. Dialect in Literature

Chapter Ten of the textbook provides much discussion about dialects. Dialects may show differences in pronunciation, grammar, and word choice. Long before linguists began to develop methods for studying and theories for explaining dialectal differences, literary writers had been interested in representing dialect speech (see, for example, exercise 3-3 in Chapter Eight of this workbook). In this exercise, consider some words from the short story "The Star in the Valley" by Mary Noailles Murfree (in *American Women Regionalists*, ed. Judith Fetterley and Marjorie Pryse [New York: W.W. Norton and Company, 1992], 254–71). In the story, Murfree is attempting to represent the speech of "mountain folk" of Eastern Tennessee. For each word, give the phonetic spelling (in IPA) of the pronunciation you believe Murfree is trying to represent. The first is completed for you as an example.

	Dialect pronunciation
A. thar 'there'	[ðɑɹ]
B. 'tain't 'it ain't'	_____
C. an' 'and'	_____
D. 'lone 'alone'	_____
E. settlemint 'settlement'	_____

---

3 You will recall from the textbook that it is common in creoles for verbs in the present tense not to show the third person singular -s. Thus, *a luv, yu luv, hi luv, shi luv*, etc. ('I love, you love, he loves, she loves,' etc.).

F. sech 'such'   _____

G. ez 'as'   _____

H. ye 'you'   _____

I. kin 'can'   _____

J. hev 'have'   _____

K. ter[4] 'to'   _____

L. fur 'for'   _____

M. oughter 'ought to'   _____

N. git 'get'   _____

OE. air 'are'   _____

---

4 The <r> in K. and M. is likely to be "silent," indicating a preceding schwa, as in <er> "uh," pronounced [ə].

PART TWO: INTERMEDIATE EXERCISES

2-1. Australian English Phonology

Consider the pronunciation of the following words in Australian English and answer the questions that follow.

tube	[tʃub]
table	[tebl̩]
tune	[tʃun]
tuck	[tʌk]
due	[dʒu]
dock	[dɔk]
duty	[dʒuti]
did	[dɪd]
assume	[əʃum]
assail	[əseil]
Sue	[ʃu]
sock	[sɔk]
presume	[prɪʒum]
preserve	[prisɜv]
zoom lens	[ʒumlɛnz]
zone	[zoun]

A. What are the two pronunciations of <t> that you observe? __[t]__ and __[tʃ]__

B. What are the two pronunciations of <d> that you observe? _____ and _____

C. What are the two pronunciations of <s> that you observe? _____ and _____

D. What are the two pronunciations of <z> that you observe? _____ and _____

E. What pattern do you see between the two pronunciations of each letter? (Hint: here it may be helpful to revisit the notion of a "natural class" from exercise 2-6 in Chapter Four).

F. Can you identify what sound appears to be the cause of the variation in pronunciation of each letter?

2-2. East Anglian English

East Anglia is located in the eastern and midland region of present-day England. It was the kingdom of East Anglia in the Anglo-Saxon Heptarchy, and for some of the Old English period had been controlled by Danes under the Danelaw.

Traditional English grammar teaches us that verbs in Present-day English are either regular or irregular, with regular verbs adding -ed to make the past tense while irregular verbs will generally change the vowel in the past tense (cf. the older distinction between weak and strong verbs). However, another way that we might classify English verbs is to count the number of forms they have for expressing the base form, the simple past, and the past participle. (These forms are known as the three principal parts of the verb.) In this way, we would note that in Standard American English, a verb like *swim, swam, swum* would have three different forms among its principal parts, while a verb like *keep, kept, kept* would have two forms. In fact, all regular verbs have two forms: *talk, talked, talked; pretend, pretended, pretended*. In this way, most verbs in English have just two forms. Finally, we might mention too that a few verbs only have one form: *hit, hit, hit*.

Consider the following principal parts list from East Anglian English and answer the questions that follow. (Based on Peter Trudgill, "The Dialect of East Anglia: Morphology, and Syntax," in *A Handbook of Varieties of English: Morphology and Syntax* [Berlin: Mouton de Gruyter, 2004], 143.)

Base Form	Past	Past Participle
begin	begun	begun
bite	bit	bit
blow	blew	blew
break	broke	broke
bring	brung	brung
catch	catched	catched
choose	chose	chose
do	done	done
draw	drawed	drawed
drink	drunk	drunk
grow	growed	growed
know	knowed	knowed
ring	rung	rung
shake	shook	shook
speak	spoke	spoke
stink	stunk	stunk
swim	swum	swum
take	took	took
teach	teached	teached
tear	tore	tore
wake	woke	woke
write	writ	writ

A. Given these verb forms, you might hear the following sentences in East Anglian English:

1. *He catched several fish at the river yesterday.*
2. *Caroline has tore her dress.*
3. *We swum in that lake every summer when I was young.*
4. *His mum and dad have spoke to him about it already.*

Looking over these forms, how do the verbs show analogical regularity?

_____

_____

B. Contrasting the set *begin, begun, begun* with Standard English, *begin, began, begun,* and the set *speak, spoke, spoke* with Standard English, *speak, spoke, spoken,* what are the two patterns of regularization among older strong verbs?

_____

_____

Can you find other examples in the set that conform to each of the patterns?

_____

_____

C. Are there any examples of former strong verbs becoming weak verbs? What are they?

_____

_____

_____

2-3. Scots English

For the data in the following exercise, see Jim Miller, "Scottish English: Morphology and Syntax," in *A Handbook of Varieties of English: Morphology and Syntax* (Berlin: Mouton de Gruyter, 2004): 47–72, at 50–51.

Consider the following pairs in which the first is a negated sentence in Scots English and the second a negated sentence in Standard English.

Scots English	Standard English
Mary's no coming.	Mary is not coming.
We'll no have enough.	We will not have enough.
The boys've no telt us otherwise.	The boys have not told us otherwise.
They're no selling wine in that store.	They are not selling wine in that store.
It'll no be too late if you do it tomorrow.	It will not be too late if you do it tomorrow.
Mike's no paid the bill yet.	Mike has not paid the bill yet.
He couldnae been here already.	He couldn't have been here already.
We didnae tell him nothing.	We didn't tell him anything.
You shouldnae been so sure.	You shouldn't have been so sure.
Jim doesnae work on Saturday.	Jim doesn't work on Saturday.
Alana cannae help you on this one.	Alana cannot help you on this one.
He mightnae be there then.	He might not be there then.

A. From the sentences above, we see that there are two patterns for negating an auxiliary in Scots English, either with *no* following the auxiliary or with *nae* contracted onto the auxiliary. Which auxiliaries are negated with *no*?

_____

_____

_____

What class of auxiliaries is negated with suffixed -*nae*?

_____

B. Based on those patterns, how would you negate the bolded parts of the following sentences in Scots English?

a. Bill **will not be** at the party.

_____

b. Frances **could not believe** what she heard.

_____

c. You and I **are not leaving** until we have finished.

_____

d. The children **should not worry** about the supplies.

_____

e. You **must not say** such awful things. (Hint: what class of auxilaries does *must* belong to?)

_____

2-4. Perfect Aspect in Irish English

In Irish English, perfect aspect can be expressed in several ways. One way is to use the verbal construction made up of the auxiliary HAVE + a past participle, a construction familiar to most varieties of English, as in *The plane has just landed*. The meaning of the perfect verb form is discussed in Chapter Two of the textbook, but we can quickly remember that the perfect signals that the verb in the HAVE + past participle construction happened in the past but is very recent, is relevant to the present time, or continues to affect the present moment. In Irish English, the first use is sometimes expressed with a construction commonly known as the "*after*-perfect." (The source of the *after*-perfect may be influence from the native Celtic Irish language.)

Here are some examples (from Jamie O'Neill, *At Swim Two Boys* [New York: Scribner, 2001]):

1. "I'm after picking up," choosily he said, "an *Irish Times* ..."
    Meaning: I have just picked up an *Irish Times*.

2. He leant over the railing. "You're after missing a spot, Nancy."
    Meaning: You have missed a spot.

3. "But you're not after forgetting it's his birthday today?"
    Meaning: But you have not forgotten it's his birthday today.

Now, consider the *have*-perfect constructions from *The Irish Times*, written in Standard English. Transform each of the *have*-perfects into the *after*-perfect equivalent.

A. Ed Joyce has announced his retirement from playing all forms of international and domestic cricket. (*IT* May 24, 2018, SPORTS)

_____

_____

B. Taoiseach Leo Varadkar said a Yes vote in Friday's referendum on the Eighth Amendment can help lift the stigma for 170,000 women who have travelled abroad to seek a termination of their pregnancy. (*IT* May 24, 2018, NEWS)

_____

_____

C. We have increased the number of nurses, doctors and therapists every year. That will continue this year. (*IT* April 7, 2019)

_____

_____

D. "The woman has been charged under the Theft and Fraud Offences Act, 2001 and will appear in court at a later date," a Garda statement said. (*IT* April 4, 2019)

_____

_____

E. The proposal has gathered momentum and, according to an opinion poll, is supported by 44 per cent of Berliners, with 39 per cent opposed. (*IT* April 7, 2019)

_____

_____

PART THREE: ADVANCED EXERCISES

3-1: Kachru's Circles of English Revisited

In exercise 1-1 of this chapter, you were asked to identify countries as occupying Kachru's inner, outer, or expanding circles depending on the status of the use of English in those countries. Considering the status of English in the countries discussed below, how might Kachru's model not account for all of the language facts in these countries?

Canada

As we read above, Canada is home to more than 90 languages, many of them Indigenous languages. Some Canadian provinces recognize Indigenous languages officially, but at the federal level only English and French are recognized.

A. _____

_____

South Africa

Not unlike the situation in Canada that we have just discussed, in South Africa English coexists with about 35 other languages. Out of that number, 11 hold official status, even though English is the de facto language used in virtually all federal capacities. One of the officially recognized languages is Afrikaans, a descendent language of Dutch, the other major European presence during the colonial period. Around 14% of the population speak Afrikaans as a first language, and geographically it can be heard in about half the country.

B. _____

_____

New Zealand

English is not recognized as an official language in New Zealand: Maori, the language of the Indigenous people of New Zealand before British colonization, is. However, less than 4% of the population can speak Maori and English is unquestionably the de facto official language. In situations like this, we say that Maori holds important symbolic status, but with less than 4% of the population able to use it, the official status serves to honor a history of the island, but not its inhabitants' linguistic practices.

C. _____

_____

3-2: The Ideology of Cartography

In Chapter Ten of the textbook, we observed how the positioning of England moved to the center of some maps as the English came to see themselves, and their language, as more central to global politics. In fact, given that the world is a 3-D spherical object, any 2-D depiction of it must involve decisions about what to place where, and those decisions will expose various ideologies about languages, cultures, geopolitical import, and the like. Consider the four maps shown below. Each of them has a different take on the distribution of countries/continents. Discuss the kinds of ideologies that seem to inform the creation of each map.

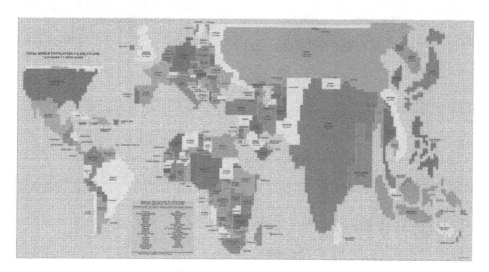

Map drawn by population size.

A. _____

_____

_____

_____

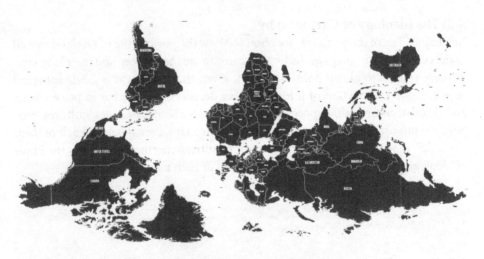

Map of the world with the Southern Hemisphere on top.

B. _____

_____

_____

_____

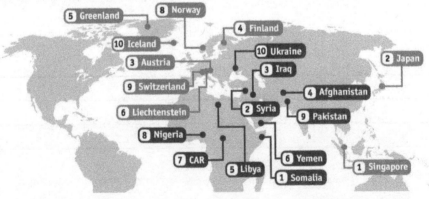

Map based on perceived security risk: black indicating high risk, gray indicating low.

C. _____

_____

_____

_____

Map showing the expression for "thank you" in the languages of the world by country
and continent: size of font is presumably related to the number of speakers.

D. _____

_____

_____

_____

3-3. Where Do Creoles Belong among the World's Languages?

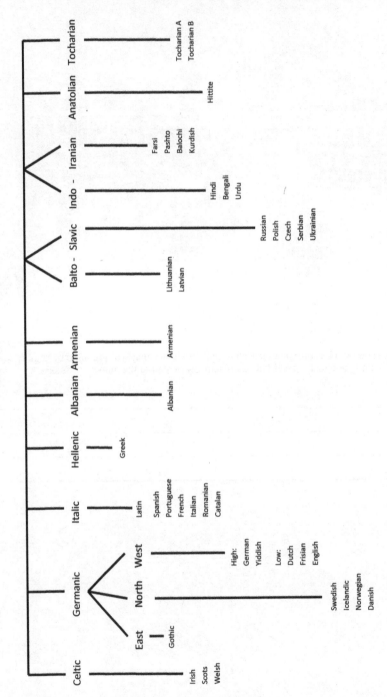

Consider the tree of Indo-European languages shown above. We have noted in the textbook that the tree exploits a pervasive metaphor that languages descend from other languages. We have called this a "genealogical" model, and we note too that some people even refer to "parent languages" or "sister languages." One interesting fact about these trees is that they rarely, if ever, include creole languages. That is, wouldn't it be fair to consider Jamaican Creole to be related to English in ways not entirely unlike the way in which Spanish is related to Latin?

A. Discuss the ways that you think the development of a creole is similar to and different from the development of Romance languages from Latin, or English and Dutch from Proto-Germanic.

_____

_____

_____

_____

B. Why do you think the genealogical metaphor is so often abandoned when discussing the developmental relationships between pidgins/creoles and their lexifier languages?

_____

_____

_____

_____

3-4. Eye Dialect

In some cases, writers capture fairly well the actual linguistic features of a dialect, but at other times it is clear that the author is imposing his/her expectation of difference even though there may be no actual difference, and is producing what is known as eye dialect. For example, sometimes to "show dialect" an author will represent a character's pronunciation of "was" as "wuz." But note that the representation "wuz" isn't really different from the Standard pronunciation [wʌz]. Eye dialect refers to the deviant spelling of a word when in fact there is no difference in the pronunciation of the word from its pronunciation in Standard English or at least a much broader and not necessarily illiterate pronunciation. Consider the passage shown below from John Steinbeck's *The Grapes of Wrath* (New York: Viking, 1939), 77-78. In that novel, Steinbeck attempts to capture the "Okie" dialect, which is essentially a South Midlands variety of American English (see the textbook, Chapter Ten).

Muley cackled. "Yeah! We're doin' somepin jus' bein' here. We're trespassin'. We can't stay. They been tryin' to catch me for two months. Now you look. If that's a car comin' we go out in the cotton an' lay down. Don't have to go far. Then by God let 'em try to fin' us! Have to look up an' down ever' row. Jus' keep your head down."

A. Which spellings do you believe actually capture a regional pronunciation and which appear to be eye dialect?

_____

_____

_____

_____

B. Do you see any inconsistencies in the presentation of "dialect" forms?

_____

_____

_____

_____

C. Are there casual English forms that are used by American English speakers generally?

_____

_____

_____

_____

Notes

Notes

Chapter One

1-1.

A. Synchronic
B. Synchronic
C. Synchronic
D. Diachronic
E. Synchronic
F. Synchronic
G. Diachronic
H. Synchronic
I. Synchronic
J. Diachronic

1-2.

A. Internal
B. External
C. Internal
D. Internal
E. External

2-1.

A. The Old English verb *willan* was replaced in Middle English by *want* as a means of expressing desire. *Will*, meanwhile, became an auxiliary verb used to express futurity.

B. Between Old and Middle English, the dual pronoun, which had referred to two and only two people, was lost.

C. Between Middle and Early Modern English, the preposition *on* in the construction-type *The king is on hunting* reduced to *a-*, yielding the form *The king is a-hunting*.

2-2.

A. It is likely that the English speakers, who were new to these areas, borrowed words from those indigenous languages for many of the plants and animals they encountered, like *banyan tree* or *skunk*.

B. It is likely that the stress at the beginning of the word left the endings on words in a weaker stress position and that they were reduced or lost over time, thus eroding grammatical information that had formerly been carried on the word.

C. It is likely that English would borrow a lot of words from Latin in precisely those areas in which Latin was used.

D. It is likely that the English spoken in these distant areas would change in ways that the English back in England did not. Additionally, it is also likely that some of the changes that took place in English in England were not picked up in the English spoken in these far-flung territories.

E. It is likely that the Old Norse language would influence the English language among those populations that had close contact with speakers of Old Norse.

F. It is likely that the most common way of signaling the grammatical meaning of plural, the *-s* in this case, would spread to other nouns for which it had not previously been used.

PART THREE: ADVANCED EXERCISES

3-1. Note: There are no right or wrong answers for this exercise at this time. It is meant as a thinking exercise that previews some of the points to be learned in the textbook. You may want to return to this exercise after reading the entire textbook to see if and how your answers have changed.

Chapter Two

PART ONE: BEGINNING EXERCISES

1-1.

A. preposition
B. noun
C. verb
D. adjective
E. adjective
F. verb
G. verb
H. noun
I. adjective
J. adverb
K. preposition
L. noun

M. verb
N. adverb
O. conjunction
P. adverb
Q. verb
R. preposition
S. noun
T. adjective
U. adverb
V. noun
W. adjective

1-2.

A. deer-irregular
B. sheep-irregular
C. men-irregular
D. eyes-regular
E. shoes-regular
F. feet-irregular

G. knives-irregular
H. cups-regular
I. mice-irregular
J. bricks-regular
K. oxen-irregular

(Note: *knives* is perhaps better thought of as a somewhat irregular plural. Clearly it takes the expected -*s*, but that -*s* causes the final *f* sound to change to a *v* sound, and that's not regular.)

1-3.

A. past perfect
B. simple past
C. simple future I progressive
D. simple future I perfect progressive
E. simple present
F. past progressive
G. present perfect progressive
H. past perfect progressive
I. simple future I
J. present progressive
K. simple future I perfect
L. present perfect

1-4.

A. larger, largest
B. bigger, biggest
C. more atrocious, most atrocious
D. colder, coldest
E. more remarkable, most remarkable
F. more circular, most circular
G. longer, longest
H. warmer, warmest
I. cuter, cutest
J. more obnoxious, most obnoxious
K. more sensitive, most sensitive

1-5.

A. subject
B. object of preposition
C. subject
D. direct object
E. object of preposition
F. subject
G. indirect object
H. direct object
I. object of preposition
J. subject
K. direct object
L. object complement
M. subject
N. subject complement
O. subject
P. object of preposition
Q. object of preposition

R. object of preposition
S. indirect object
T. direct object
U. object of preposition
V. subject
W. subject complement
X. object of preposition
Y. subject
Z. indirect object
AA. direct object
BB. object of preposition
CC. subject
DD. subject complement
EE. object of preposition
FF. object of preposition

PART TWO: INTERMEDIATE EXERCISES

2-1.

A. definite article
B. noun
C. lexical verb
D. adverb
E. preposition
F. noun
G. adverb
H. adjective
I. adjective
J. subordinate conjunction
K. lexical verb
L. preposition
M. demonstrative determiner
N. noun
O. auxiliary verb
P. coordinate conjunction
Q. adverb
R. indefinite article
S. adjective

T. possessive determiner
U. preposition
V. adverb
W. subordinate conjunction
X. personal pronoun
Y. demonstrative determiner
Z. auxiliary verb
AA. preposition
BB. noun
CC. personal pronoun
DD. auxiliary verb
EE. lexical verb
FF. subordinate conjunction
GG. preposition
HH. possessive pronoun
II. personal pronoun
JJ. indefinite pronoun
KK. demonstrative determiner

2-2.

A. noun-I have a crush on Rick Springfield. / verb-The wrecking ball crushed the concrete wall.
B. preposition-The cat ran up the tree. / verb-The gambler upped the ante.
C. noun-The store hung up a new sign. / verb-We signed the contract yesterday.
D. preposition-My mother shoo'ed the cat out the door. / verb-The magazine outed the well-known actor.
E. adjective-The floor was not level. / verb-The new rules were meant to level the playing field.
F. adjective-The ball was too light to pass. / verb-The scouts have to light the fire each night.
G. noun-I sat in the big chair. / verb-Alexandra chaired the meeting.
H. adjective-That was the best macaroni and cheese I have ever had! / verb-The athlete bested his own record in the tournament.

I. noun-Release the hounds! / verb-Jacob's past hounded him throughout the election.
J. adverb-Please move your seat forward. / verb-I forwarded the email to my co-worker.

(Note that some answers may vary. The answers offered here are a guide. For instance, while this answer key offers adjective and verb for the word *light*, it may also be a noun, as in "Do you have a light?")

2-3.

A. syllabi
B. hooves
C. alumnae
D. addenda
E. diagnoses

F. appendices
G. cacti
H. halves
I. matrices
J. wharves

(Note that the plurals given here follow very prescriptive rules, many of which can only be considered pedantic in modern times. The point of the exercise is to observe that despite prescriptive rules, speakers follow different patterns or are unsure of the pattern they "should" follow.)

2-4.

A. them
B. our
C. he
D. your
E. me

F. they
G. my
H. her
I. us
J. it

2-5.

A. My cell phone was replaced (by the company)...
B. Your package has been left on the back patio of your house (by the driver).
C. The inmates were being transferred to a new cell block (by the guards)...
D. The dish is made with many ingredients (by the cook)...
E. The board had been erased (by someone)...
F. Resources are being compiled (by researchers)...
G. Four new relay towers have been installed throughout the state (by the company).

(Note that the agent of each passive is included in parentheses because it is grammatically optional. Without more context, we can't really know if it is desirable to express it or not.)

2-6.

A. modal-permission

B. modal-ability

C. modal-suggestion

D. quasi-modal-permission

E. quasi-modal-obligation

F. modal-suggestion

G. quasi-modal-obligation/necessity

H. quasi-modal-obligation

I. quasi-modal-ability

J. modal-obligation

K. modal-permission

2-7.

A. sunnier/sunniest

B. handsomer/handsomest

C. tenderer/tenderest

D. livelier/liveliest

E. awesomer/awesomest

F. nimbler/nimblest

G. crappier/crappiest

H. cleverer/cleverest

(Note that the forms given here follow very prescriptive rules, many of which can only be considered pedantic in modern times. The point of the exercise is to observe that despite prescriptive rules, speakers follow different patterns or are unsure of the pattern they "should" follow.)

2-8.

A. subject

B. direct object

C. direct object

D. subject

E. direct object

F. indirect object

G. direct object

H. subject complement

I. subject

J. direct object

K. object complement

L. subject

M. direct object

N. object of preposition

O. subject complement

P. object of preposition

Q. subject

R. direct object

S. direct object

T. indirect object

U. direct object

V. subject

W. direct object

X. object of preposition

Y. object of preposition

Z. object of preposition

AA. subject

BB. direct object

CC. direct object

DD. direct object

EE. object of preposition

FF. object of preposition

GG. subject

HH. object of preposition

II. subject complement

JJ. direct object

KK. object of preposition

LL. object of preposition

MM. direct object

NN. object of preposition

OO. object of preposition

2-9.
A. compound-complex
B. simple
C. complex
D. simple
E. compound-complex
F. simple
G. complex
H. complex
I. simple

2-10.
A. that, Ø
B. who, that
C. which
D. who
E. who(m), that, Ø
F. whom
G. who(m)
H. that, Ø
I. whom
J. who, that

(It is possible that responses may vary depending on various factors—formality, dialect, age, etc. The answers given here accord with the rules of Standard American English.)

2-11.
A. direct object
B. subject
C. object of preposition
D. direct object
E. subject complement
F. subject
G. direct object
H. subject complement
I. direct object
J. subject

2-12.
A. time
B. concession
C. cause
D. condition
E. time
F. cause
G. condition
H. place
I. time

PART THREE: ADVANCED EXERCISES

3-1.
A. The children are read fairy tales (by Mr. Suzuki) every Saturday in the library./
   Fairy tales are read to the children (by Mr. Suzuki) every Saturday in the library.
B. The public were not shown the recount numbers (by the election committee).../
   The recount numbers were not shown to the public (by the election committee)...
C. We were sold the wrong tickets (by the theater).../The wrong tickets were sold

to us (by the theater)...

D. Each retiree will be provided a comprehensive package (by the human resources department).../A comprehensive package will be provided to each retiree (by the human resources department)...

E. All of the delegates should be presented a welcome in their own language (by the welcoming committee)./A welcome in their own language should be presented to all of the delegates (by the welcoming committee).

F. The office was delivered all of the items ordered (by Gabor).../All of the items ordered were delivered to the office (by Gabor)...

G. His cabinet had been told lies (by the President).../Lies had been told to his cabinet (by the President)...

H. Mrs. McGillicuddy was handed the essays (by the children).../The essays were handed to Mrs. McGillicuddy (by the children)...

I. Mia should be passed the ball (by Logan).../The ball should be passed to Mia (by Logan)...

3-2. While there could be some variation in responses, a typical arrangement for speakers of North American English would likely be (in descending order): will-must-would-should-could-may-might.

3-3. Answers here will vary considerably. Essentially the issue is that native English words, like *brittle*, probably sound more acceptable with -*er*/-*est* to more speakers of English than do words from other languages, like *macho*.

3-4.
A. adjective
B. noun
C. noun
D. noun
E. noun
F. noun
G. adjective
H. adjective
I. noun
J. adjective

3-5.
A. who-subject
B. Ø-object of preposition
C. which-subject
D. who-direct object
E. which-object of preposition
F. that-direct object
G. that-subject
H. Ø-direct object
I. that-object of preposition
J. Ø-direct object
K. who-object of preposition

(Note that Ø indicates a deleted relative pronoun.)

3-6.

A. His resume did not clearly indicate where Alan finished his degree.

B. The child asked whether (or if) the cookies were ready.

C. That (or the fact that) our car gets approximately 40 miles to a gallon of gas will save us several hundred dollars each year.

D. The founders of the new country debated where the capitol would be located.

E. Song-Ha saw that the television had been moved from its usual position.

F. That (or the fact that) the second edition of the book had been released necessitated a change in the cataloguing system.

G. Moriki enjoyed that (or the fact that) Aaron played his flute on the patio before dinner.

H. The students wondered when the first day of class was.

I. No one is quite certain if (or whether) the city collects yard debris on Tuesdays.

J. The students didn't like that (or the fact that) they were only given two days to read the entire novel.

K. Kollandra asked me if (or whether) the coffee shop had raised its prices after Christmas.

(You will note that in a few answers the verb form has been changed to a past or past perfect in the case that the main verb was in the past. This is in keeping with the sequencing of tenses recommended in most handbooks on Standard English.)

Chapter Three

1-1. For the answers, please consult a political map of present-day Europe.

1-2.
A.   d…k
B.   p…d
C.   t…s
D.   n…p…t
E.   m…t…r

(Note that the forms should be completed based on the consonant that the majority of languages show for that position in the word indicated.)

1-3.
A. Angolan—borrowed from the enslaved Africans of the American south/Caribbean who spoke languages from Angola
B. Name of a city in India—borrowed because cloth with a calico pattern was exported from that port
C. Greek—borrowed along with the liquor of the same name
D. Italian—borrowed because of the importance of the Italian language in the history of Western music
E. Italian—also borrowed because of the importance of the Italian language in Western music
F. Latin—borrowed because of the use of Latin in matters of law and administration
G. Polynesian—borrowed as European colonists became familiar with (and perhaps intrigued by) religious systems that they encountered on certain of the Pacific islands

1-4.

A. These seem to be cognates since Dutch and English descend from the same parent language and share a lot of core vocabulary.

B. These seem to be a case of borrowing from Japanese into English since English and Japanese are not related languages.

C. These seem to be cognates since English and German descend from the same parent language and share a lot of core vocabulary.

D. These seem to be a case of borrowing from English since English and Chinese are not related languages.

E. These seem to be cognates since English and Spanish descend from a common ancestor.

F. These seem to be a case of borrowing from Turkish into English, since English and Turkish are not related languages.

G. These seem to be a case of borrowing from Hebrew into English likely influenced by the importance of Hebrew as a biblical language.

H. These seem to be cognates since Russian and English descend from a common ancestor language.

I. These seem to be cognates since Bengali and English share a common ancestor language.

J. These seem to be a case of borrowing into English from Narragansett, probably as a result of contact between Native American groups and early settlers in North America.

1-5.

A. frail is older.

B. crown is older.

C. delight is older.

D. dainty is older.

E. school is older.

In general we can note that the older borrowings tend to be borrowed into English from Latin via French and thus reflect spellings from Old French. Also, the more recently borrowed words are closer to their Latin forms, for example Eng. *Coronation* ~ Lat. *corona*, a fact that correlates with their often having more syllables than the earlier-borrowed words.

1-6.

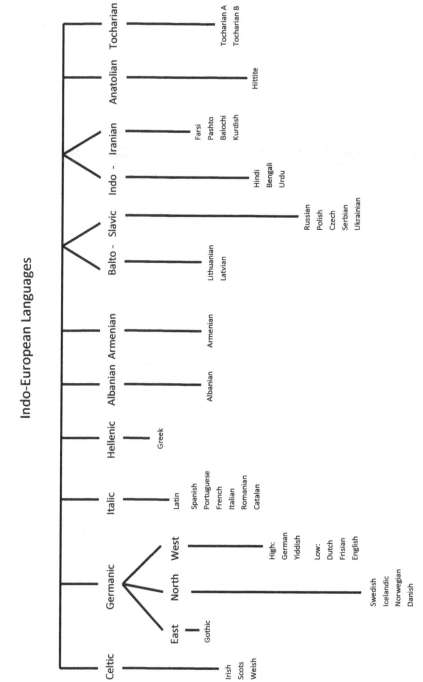

Indo-European Languages

Celtic
  Irish
  Scots
  Welsh

Germanic
  East
    Gothic
  North
    Swedish
    Icelandic
    Norwegian
    Danish
  West
    High:
      German
      Yiddish
    Low:
      Dutch
      Frisian
      English

Italic
  Latin
  Spanish
  Portuguese
  French
  Italian
  Romanian
  Catalan

Hellenic
  Greek

Albanian
  Albanian

Armenian
  Armenian

Balto - Slavic
  Lithuanian
  Latvian
  Russian
  Polish
  Czech
  Serbian
  Ukrainian

Indo - Iranian
  Indo -
    Hindi
    Bengali
    Urdu
  Iranian
    Farsi
    Pashto
    Balochi
    Kurdish

Anatolian
  Hittite

Tocharian
  Tocharian A
  Tocharian B

1-7.

A. X, A, O

B. X, O, P

C. X, P, X, P, P

D. P, X, O, P

E. X, P, O, O

F. X, X, P, X

G. A, O, P

H. X, X, P

I. X, O, P, P, P

J. X, O, O

K. X, A, O, P

PART TWO: INTERMEDIATE EXERCISES

2-1. For the answers, please consult a political map of present-day Europe and Asia and the list of languages spoken by country at the Ethnologue website (www.ethnologue. com).

2-2.

A. <u>The beginning [f] of Vulgar Latin appears to have been deleted in Spanish.</u>

B. The consonant cluster [pl] has changed to [pj] in Italian.

C. The [b] between vowels in Vulgar Latin has changed to [β] in Spanish.

D. The [b] between vowels in Vulgar Latin has changed into [β] in Spanish (as in C.)/the [b] in Vulgar Latin has changed to [v] in Italian and Portuguese.

E. Beginning [bl] in Vulgar Latin has changed into [bj] in Italian.

F. The final [e] in Vulgar Latin has been deleted in Spanish/the [n] in Vulgar Latin has changed to [ɲ] in Portuguese/the [m] in Vulgar Latin has changed to [mm] in Italian, which represents a long pronunciation of [m].

G. The [s] in Vulgar Latin has changed to [z] in Portuguese and Italian.

H. The [s] in Vulgar Latin has changed to [z] in Portuguese and Italian (as in G.)/ the [o] in Vulgar Latin has changed to [oi] in Portuguese.

I. The [e] in Vulgar Latin has changed to [je] in Spanish.

J. The [t] in Vulgar Latin has changed to [d] in Spanish and Portuguese/the [e] in Vulgar Latin has changed into [je] in Spanish and Italian.

2-3.

A. The words have to do with tropical Island *life*, *canoe/sand/flower*, or with basic human terms, *man/woman*.

B. These are words that would resist interference (borrowing) from other languages and they are words that would have been present most likley in the parent language.

C. You would not expect to find words for things like 'snow,' 'reindeer,' or 'evergreen.'

2-4.
A.   French[1]
B.   Latin
C.   Modern Latin
D.   Norse[2]
E.   Unknown
F.   Italian
G.   Latin and Greek

The words in this list probably seem more "native" somehow than the words in 1-4. The reason for this is that they are more common and in many cases have been in the language longer. Additionally, they are not "culture-bound" in the same way words like *shish kebab* or *cherub* are.

2-5.
A. with-*with* comes from Old English but is odd because it now so strongly signals accompaniment while its original meaning is 'against.' How does something meaning 'against' come to mean 'together'?
B. teleprompter-*tele* is a prefix developed from Greek meaning "far" and used in a number of scientific/technological words, for example *telephone*, *telescope*, etc. But the *prompter* part is native English, from the verb *prompt*. Thus the word is very deliberately created and created partly from native stock and partly borrowed stock.
C. rich-*rich* has two possible etymologies from two very different sources. One is from the common Germanic stock, in which case it is thought to be related to the German word *Reich*, meaning power/authority. The other possibility is a French origin with the meaning of 'abundant.' The *OED* suggests that it may be both.
D. gain-according to the *OED* the word was originally borrowed from Norse and then became obsolete, but then was later borrowed again from French in the 15th century.
E. courtship-it is a hybrid word in that the *court-* part of the word is borrowed from French, but the suffix *-ship* is a native English suffix.

2-6. The words in list A represent the newer borrowings and the words in B represent the older borrowing. This is somewhat obvious because the words in A are closer in form to the Latin original and the words in B show more effects of sound changes that have happened in Spanish during its history.

---

1 Note that the *OED* gives the origin as Anglo-Norman, which was a dialect of French.
2 Note that the *OED* gives the origin as "early Scandinavian," which we refer to here and in the book as (Old) Norse, although the specialist in historical Germanic linguistics will consider them distinct in some ways.

PART THREE: ADVANCED EXERCISES

3-1. There is no right answer for this exercise.

3-2. For the answers, please consult a political map of the present-day world and the list of languages spoken by country at the Ethnologue website (www.ethnologue. com).

3-3.
A. It seems clear that the proto-word would begin with [f] and then a high vowel, probably [i]. After that, it seems likely that the next sound would be a nasal, perhaps [n] and then a labio-dental. So something like [finf]. English appears to the phonetically most deviant of the set.
B. The proto-word is likely to be something like [hopen], given that the majority of languages have [hop(e)]. Although only two of the languages have a final [-n], it is more likely that a final [-n] would drop off than be added. If this reconstruction is right, German appears to have changed the most radically, shifting [p] to [f]. This change in fact did happen in German and is known as one of the changes in the Second Germanic Sound Shift.
C. The proto-word very likely began with [t] and then a low vowel, which is difficult to determine from this set. The final sound that we could posit is a final nasal, but note that English doesn't show that. In fact the proto-word is something like [tonθ]. Although this information would not be recoverable from just these data, English lost nasals in such environments before fricatives and the other languages lost the fricative. The shift of German [t] to [ts] is also part of the Second Germanic Sound Shift referred to in the answer to B.
D. The likely proto-word here is straightforwardly [ik] or something close to it. Danish shows the largest departure from that posited form and the shift of German [k] to [ç] is also part of the Second Germanic Sound Shift referred to in the answers to B and C.

Chapter Four

1-1.
A. 5
B. 1
C. 6
D. 2
E. 3
F. 7
G. 9
H. 10
I. 8
J. 4

1-2.
A. 6
B. 1
C. 10
D. 3
E. 8
F. 5
G. 9
H. 2
I. 7
J. 4

1-3.
A. 5
B. 10
C. 1
D. 7
E. 6
F. 9
G. 3
H. 8
I. 4
J. 2

1-4.
A. [æ]
B. [u]
C. [ʌ]
D. [oi]
E. [ʊ]
F. [ɑi]
G. [ɑ]
H. [e]
I. [ɛ]
J. [o]
K. [ɔ]
L. [ə]
M. [i]
N. [ɑu]
O. [ɪ]

1-5.

A. rich
B. pen
C. think
D. every
E. lash
F. look
G. smoke
H. feel
I. rack
J. cut

K. take
L. shoot
M. astounding
N. really
O. taught
P. crave
Q. shed
R. adjust
S. cage
T. siding

1-6.

A. [sæt]
B. [mek]
C. [fɔl]
D. [ɹʌʃ]
E. [tʃip]
F. [lɛft]
G. [bɹud]
H. [pʊt]
I. [dɹaiv]
J. [laus]

K. [tait]
L. [fjul]
M. [dʒoi]
N. [bes]
O. [wʊd]
P. [əwek]
Q. [bɪtwin]
R. [flʌd]
S. [sɪntæks]
T. [sɪti]

PART TWO: INTERMEDIATE EXERCISES

2-1.

A. [tʃɛɹ] / [tʃeɹ]
B. [ɹoɹ] /[ɹoɹ]
C. [paɹt] / [pɔɹt]
D. [eɹəɹ] / [ɛɹəɹ]
E. [bɝn]
F. [iɹ] / [ɪɹ]
G. [feɹ] / [fɛɹ]
H. [ɝn]
I. [kwaɹt] / [kwoɹt] / [kwɔɹt]

2-2.

A. --- / stress on second syllable
B. tap / stress on first syllable
C. tap / stress on first syllable
D. tap / stress on first syllable
E. --- / stress on second syllable

F. tap / stress on first syllable
G. --- / stress on second syllable
H. tap / stress on the first syllable
I. tap / stress on the first syllable
J. tap / stress on the first syllable

K. tap / stress on the first syllable
L. --- / stress on the second syllable
M. tap / stress on the first syllable
N. --- / stress on the second syllable
O. --- / stress on the second syllable

P. tap / stress on the first syllable
Q. --- / stress on the second syllable
R. --- / stress on the second syllable
S. tap / stress on the first syllable
T. tap / stress on the first syllable

You should recognize that tapping occurs after a stressed syllable and not when stress follows the alveolar stop.

2-3.
A. [bærəl]
B. [ærɪk]
C. [ətɑmɪk]
D. [motɛl]
E. [ɹɪdus]
F. [lɛrɚ]
G. [lærɚ]
H. [əton]
I. [miɾi]
J. [ədu]

2-4.
A. [ɹɑiɾɨ]
B. [mɪtn̩]
C. [bærl̩]
D. [lɪɾɨ]
E. [kʌɾl̩]
F. [bʌtn̩]
G. [ekɹ]
H. [ʃʌvl̩]
I. [lætn̩] (Note that as in B. and F. in most American English pronunciations of this word what we have represented here with [t] will actually be a glottal stop.)
J. [ɛvɹ]

2-5.
A. The two words contrast in final position, a. containing a voiceless interdental fricative and b. a voiced interdental fricative.
B. The two words contrast in initial position, a. containing a voiced bilabial nasal and b. a voiceless velar stop.
C. The two words contrast in medial position, a. containing a low back lax vowel [ɑ] and b. a low front lax vowel [æ].
D. The two words contrast in initial position, a. containing a voiced alveolar lateral and b. a voiceless alveopalatal fricative.
E. The two words contrast in final position, a. containing a voiced alveolar nasal and b. a voiced velar stop.
F. The two words contrast in initial position, a. containing a high front lax vowel [ɪ] and b. a low front lax vowel [e].
G. The two words contrast in final position, a. containing a voiceless velar stop and b. a voiced bilabial stop.

H. The two words contrast in initial position, a. containing a voiceless bilabial stop and b. a voiced alveolar stop.
I. The two words contrast in final position, a. containing a voiceless velar stop and b. a voiceless alveopalatal fricative.
J. The two words contrast in final position, a. containing a high front tense vowel [i] and b. a high back tense vowel [u].
K. The two words contrast in final position, a. containing a voiced velar stop and b. a voiced alveopalatal affricate.

2-6.

A. The three sounds all share the feature of having a velar articulation.
B. The three sounds all share the feature of having a voiceless stop articulation.
C. The three sounds all share the feature of having a nasal articulation.
D. The three sounds all share the feature of being high vowels.
E. The three sounds all share the feature of having a voiced articulation.
F. The three sounds all share the feature of being mid vowels.
G. The three sounds all share the feature of having a fricative articulation.
H. The three sounds all share the feature of having an alveolar articulation.
I. The three sounds all share the feature of having a velar articulation.
J. The three sounds all share the feature of being back vowels.
K. The three sounds all share the feature of having a voiced articulation.

PART THREE: ADVANCED EXERCISES

3-1.

A. The alveolar [n] in the word "can" in the first sentence has changed to a velar [ŋ] and the vowel [u] in "you" in the first sentence has changed to a schwa, [ə].
B. The [ɹ] in *worked* has become syllabic and the [t] in that same word has deleted.
C. The [ɝ] in *learned* has become syllabic and the final [d] has deleted. Also, the second to last vowel has deleted in the word *elementary*.
D. The [t] in *what* has combined with the [j] in [ju] to become a voiceless alveopalatal fricative [tʃ].
E. The [t] in the word *pet* has become a glottal stop [ʔ] and the word *hamster* has added a [p] between [m] and [s].

3-2.

A. The alveolar [n] in the first sentence has changed into the bilabial [m] in assimilation with the following bilabial [m] in *made*.

B. The alveolar [d] in *would* has become the alveopalatal [dʒ] because of the palatal [j] in *you*. Note that this kind of "palatalization" before [j] or high vowels like [u] or [i] is very common in the languages of the world.

C. The alveolar [s] in *miss* has become an alveopalatal [ʃ] in anticipation of the palatal [j] in *you* (again a very common assimilatory process).

D. The alveolar [n] in *ongoing* has become the velar [ŋ] in assimilation with the following velar [g] in the same word.

E. The alveolar [z] in *knows* has become the alveopalatal [ʒ] in anticipation of the palatal [j] in *you*, which is similar to the change in B and C of this exercise.

F. The alveolar [t] in *meet* has become alveopalatal [tʃ] in anticipation of the palatal [j] in *you*. Compare B, C, and E in this exercise.

3-3. The solution to this problem is that voiceless stops aspirate or carry a puff of air when they are word initial or when they occur before a stressed syllable.

ANSWERS

Chapter Five

1-1.

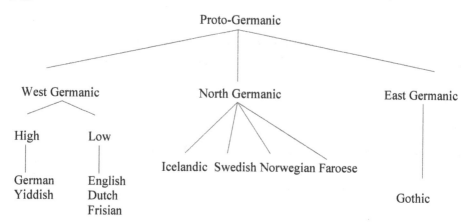

1-2.

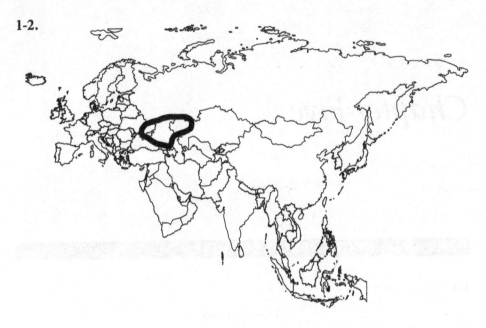

The area circled here represents the area that most scholars (but not all!) agree to be the homeland of the speakers of Proto-Indo-European.

1-3.

Indo-European		Germanic
A. Voiceless Stops	>	Voiceless Fricatives
p	>	f
t̯	>	θ
k	>	x/h
B. Voiced Stops	>	Voiceless Stops
b̲	>	p
d̲	>	t
g	>	k̲
C. Aspirated Voiced Stops	>	Unaspirated Voiced Stops
bh	>	b̲
dh̲	>	d
gh	>	g

1-4.

A. weak
B. strong
C. weak
D. weak
E. strong
F. weak
G. strong
H. strong
I. weak
J. weak
K. weak
L. strong

M. strong
N. weak
O. strong
P. weak
Q. strong
R. weak
S. weak
T. weak
U. strong
V. strong
W. strong

PART TWO: INTERMEDIATE EXERCISES

2-1. The five features of Germanic languages are (the answers need not be in this order):
A. Fixed initial stress on the word root
B. A system of strong and weak adjectives
C. A two-tense system (simple present and simple past)
D. A system of strong and weak verbs. Examples will vary.
E. Grimm's Law

2-2.

Text One: *is, feels, have, succeeded, mastering, are, leave, have, learned, playing, heard, have, achieved, works, is, put, can, must, include, have, achieving, is, document, receive, is, show, has, helped, contribute, would, regard.*

Text Two: *did, worked, did, started, served, 's, is, wasn't, was, was, started, were, paid.*

A. The most frequent verb form is some form of *have* as an auxiliary in the first text and some form of *be* in the second.
B. Forms of *be* are the second most frequent in Text One and *did* and *started* are the second most frequent verbs in Text Two.
C. In Text One, and counting only finite verbs, there are 8 synthetic verb forms and 6 periphrastic verb forms, whereas there is one periphrastic form in Text Two.
D. The different frequency can be accounted for in terms of genre and style. Text One is academic prose, and more complex verb forms are more common because writers have more time to plan how they want to express their ideas. Text Two is a spoken text in which we commonly find fewer periphrastic verb forms and a large number of forms of the verb *be*.

PART THREE: ADVANCED EXERCISES

3-1.
A. strong
B. weak
C. weak
D. strong
E. weak
F. strong

3-2. This is a "thinking" exercise and the point is to generate ideas. There are no fixed answers for the exercise.

Chapter Six

1-1.

A. The answers will vary but the pattern that initial /k/ is aspirated at the beginning of a word and not aspirated after [s] will hold true for whatever examples are produced.

B. The answers will vary but the pattern that initial /k/ is aspirated at the beginning of a word and not aspirated after [s] will hold true for whatever examples are produced even though the words are invented.

1-2.

A. X and Y are in complementary distribution because X never occurs in a position that Y does.

B. X and Y are not in complementary distribution because, at least in some cases, they occur in the same position among the letters in the two columns, for example IXV and IYV, or at the beginning of the sequence followed by O, XO... and YO....

1-3. (The answers need not be in this particular order)

A. rife-ripe- contrasting sounds /f/ and /p/

B. soup-coup- contrasting sounds /s/ and /k/

C. fat-fab- contrasting sounds /t/ and /b/

D. hair-bear- contrasting sounds /h/ and /b/

E. pale-shale- contrasting sounds /p/ and /ʃ/

F. song-long- contrasting sounds /s/ and /l/

G. four-poor- contrasting sounds /f/ and /p/

H. zip-sip- contrasting sounds /z/ and /s/

I. shut-shove- contrasting sounds /t/ and /v/

1-4.

A. Minimal Pair: leisure and leader. Contrasting sounds: /ʒ/ and /d/. Contrast location: second consonant of the words

B. Minimal Pair: tear and fair. Contrasting sounds: /t/ and /f/. Contrast location: first sound of the words

C. Minimal Pair: sing and song. Contrasting sounds: /ɪ/ and /ɔ/. Contrast location: second sound of the words

D. Minimal Pair: alone and atone. Contrasting sounds: /l/ and /t/. Contrast location: second sound of the words

E. Minimal Pair: took and book. Contrasting sounds: /t/ and /b/. Contrast location: first sound of the words

F. Minimal Pair: low and go. Contrasting sounds: /l/ and /g/. Contrast location: first sound of the words

G. Minimal Pair: arm and art. Contrasting sounds: /m/ and /t/. Contrast location: final sound of the words

H. Minimal Pair: cluck and club. Contrasting sounds: /k/ and /b/. Contrast location: final sound of the words

I. Minimal Pair: reek and rack. Contrasting sounds: /i/ and /æ/. Contrast location: second sound of the words

J. Minimal Pair: braid and brood. Contrasting sounds: /e/ and /u/. Contrast location: third sound of the words

K. Minimal Pair: thy and thigh. Contrasting sounds: /ð/ and /θ/. Contrast location: first sound of the words

L. Minimal Pair: abyss and amiss. Contrasting sounds: /b/ and /m/. Contrast location: second sound of the words

M. Minimal Pair: lack and leak. Contrasting sounds: /æ/ and /i/. Contrast location: second sound of the words

1-5.

A. [ɱ] occurs before labiodental sounds, [f] and [v].

B. [n̪] occurs before interdental sounds, [θ] and [ð].

C. [ŋ] occurs before velar sounds, [k] and [g].

D. [n] occurs before vowels.

1-6. [z] occurs before voiced consonants and [s] occurs everywhere else. (Note that while it may seem like a "cop-out" to say simply that [s] occurs everywhere else, this is actually the correct way to describe the pattern. It is easy to state the more limited occurrence of [z], but [s] has a much more varied distribution.)

1-7. Examples will vary, but the inflectional and derivational status of each is:
A. *-s* is inflectional and *-ity* is derivational
B. *-dom* is derivational and *-ing* is inflectional
C. *-ed* is inflectional and *-al* is derivational
D. *-s* is inflectional and *-ic* is derivational

PART TWO: INTERMEDIATE EXERCISES

2-1. The answers here will vary.

2-2. Sonorants devoice when they follow a voiceless stop.

2-3. The phoneme /t/ in Japanese can be realized as either [t] or [tʃ]. [tʃ] occurs before [i] and [t] occurs everywhere else.

2-4.
A. A prefix, bi-, has been added to the word. The prefix appears to be derivational since it has the effect of creating a new word.
B. -e is suffixed to the verb to express a first person singular (I) subject. It is likely inflectional since it does not create a new word but a grammatical form of the verb.
C. The prefix ni- is added to the word to add the sense of deprivation. It is likely derivational since it has the effect of creating a new word.
D. The suffix -ku has been added to the word to make the accusative form of the word. It is likely inflectional since it does not create a new word but a grammatical form of the noun.
E. -khana has been suffixed (compounded) to the word to create a new word. Since the effect is the creation of a new word, the process is derivational.
F. -mane has been suffixed to the word to create the plural. Since it creates a new grammatical form of the word, it is most likely inflectional.
G. -mi has been suffixed to the word to create a noun from an adjective. Since it created a new word in a new word class, it is derivational.
H. The morpheme -akt- has been infixed into the adjective to create a noun. Since it created a new word in a new word class, it is derivational.
I. -ib has been suffixed to the word to create the future tense. Since it has the effect of creating a new grammatical form of the word, it is likely inflectional.

PART THREE: ADVANCED EXERCISES

3-1.

A. [h] occurs at the beginning of a word and [ŋ] before [g] or [k]. (Actually [h] may occur in the middle of words like *mishap* or *cohere*, but always before a stressed syllable and never before [g] or [k].) The two sounds are in complementary distribution.

B. Although the sounds are in complementary distribution, it would not be a sound linguistic analysis to consider them allophones of the same phoneme because they are phonetically too different.

3-2.

A. Minimal Pair *ata* and *ota*. Contrasting sounds /a/ and /o/.

B. Minimal Pair *veha* and *vepa*. Contrasting sounds /h/ and /p/.

C. Minimal Pair *haita* and *haiti*. Contrasting sounds /a/ and /i/.

D. Minimal Pair *chaya* and *maya*. Contrasting sounds /tʃ/ and /m/.

E. Minimal Pair *yeeka* and *yeecha*. Contrasting sounds /k/ and /tʃ/.

F. Minimal Pair *omta* and *omna*. Contrasting sounds /t/ and /n/.

G. Minimal Pair *haaka* and *naaka*. Contrasting sounds /h/ and /n/.

3-3.

A. The words in column A are devoiced and those in column B are less devoiced or not devoiced at all.

B. The stronger devoicing happens when the consonant cluster involving a voiceless stop and a sonorant is before a stressed syllable.

3-4.

A. 1. [æ] 2. [ə]
B. 1. [e] 2. [ə]
C. 1. [e] 2. [ə]
D. 1. [e] 2. [ə]
E. 1. [ɛ] 2. [ə]

F. 1. [ɑ] 2. [ə]
G. 1. [ɛ] 2. [ə]
H. 1. [æ] 2. [ə]
I. 1. [ɛ] 2. [ə]
J. 1. [ɑ] 2. [ə]

The syllables in the B list all tend towards schwa (or sometimes [ɪ] depending on how careful one's pronunciation is. This happens when the stress shifts to another syllable leaving the vowel in an unstressed syllable.)

3-5. English and German are alike in that they aspirate voiceless consonants before a stressed syllable in a word. Dutch, however, does not follow the same phonological pattern. (Note that the phonetics here represent the standard dialects of Dutch, English, and German. There is variation on this matter in dialects of the languages in question.)

3-6. This is a thinking exercise and the answers become apparent as one works through the textbook. For A. you will learn that in older varieties of English, there were several ways to make a noun plural. Present-day exceptions are usually those surviving older patterns. For B. the class of verbs known as modal verbs doesn't take -s: can, could, will, would, may, might, shall, should, and must. Their form is due to the fact that those verbs developed as a set of auxiliary verbs very early in English from earlier past tense forms and thus don't have the present third person singular -s marked on them.

3-7. The examples here will vary, but you will notice that the native suffixes tend not to cause changes in the stem and the removal of the suffix will nearly always result in a free base or root. For example, *king-kingdom*. The non-native stems often involve changes in the stem (for example *magic-magician*, which changes in the stress and final consonant) and sometimes removal of the suffix yields a base that is not a free lexical morpheme, that is, not a word (for example *ammunition*).

Chapter Seven

1-1.

A. path
B. English
C. shilling
D. hedge
E. ditch
F. thorn
G. day
H. sorry
I. fast
J. witchcraft
K. thickness
L. thankful

1-2.

A. That is his ship
B. (A) Fish was in water
C. That child is evil
D. (A) Spellbook was heavy
E. (A) Smith drank milk
F. He was crafty

1-3.

A. Fine ladies had famous chefs
B. Famous chefs hired crooked assistants
C. Crooked assistants adored fine ladies
D. Crooked assistants adored fine ladies
E. Famous chefs gave fine ladies nervous lapdogs
F. Fine ladies gave crooked assistants nervous lapdogs

1-4.

A. The man loved the dog
B. The lord loved the king
C. The king loved the shipman
D. The shipman loved the dog
E. The dog loved the lord

1-5.

A. 2nd, "you"
B. 2nd, "you"
C. 3rd, "he/she/it"
D. 1st, "I"
E. 2nd, "you"
F. 3rd, "he/she/it"
G. 3rd, "he/she/it"
H. 2nd, "you"
I. 1st, "I"
J. 3rd, "he/she/it"
K. 2nd, "you"
L. 1st, "I"
M. 1st, "I"
N. 2nd, "you"
O. 3rd, "he/she/it"

1-6.

A. baptismal font
B. divinity
C. evangelist
D. celestial
E. manna
F. astronomer
G. partaking of the Eucharist
H. passion
I. martyrdom
J. martyrology
K. unicorn
L. testament

1-7. Answers will vary

PART TWO: INTERMEDIATE EXERCISES

2-1.

A. *þǣre*, feminine genitive singular and *þǣre*, feminine dative singular
B. *þæs*, masuline genitive singular and *þæs*, neuter genitive singular
C. *þone*, masculine accusative singular
D. *þǣm*, masculine dative singular, *þǣm* neuter dative singular, and *þǣm*, all genders dative plural
E. *þāra*, all genders genitive plural
F. nominative and accusative
G. genitive and dative
H. nominative and accusative
I. nominative and accusative

2-2.
A. þis
B. þisses
C. þisse
D. þissum
E. þissum
F. þās
G. þās

2-3.
A. þæs
B. þone
C. þāra
D. þǣm
E. þǣm
F. þǣre
G. þone
H. þāra
I. þǣm
J. þǣm

2-4.
A. genitive
B. plural
C. plural

2-5.
A. singular
B. plural
C. singular
D. plural
E. singular
F. plural
G. plural
H. singular

2-6.
A. *þā Deniscan lēode* is the subject of the verb *fērdon*
B. *sciphere* is the object of the preposition *mid*
C. *þǣm flotan* is the object of the preposition *on*
D. *dēofol* is the object of the preposition *þurh*
E. *þæt land* is the direct object of the verb *āwēston*
F. *scipum* is the object of the preposition *mid*
G. *wælhrēonesse* is the object of the preposition *mid*
H. *West-seaxna* is in the genitive because it indicates a relationship like possession (note that we would translate it as "of the West-Saxons")
I. *se foresægda Hinguar* is the subject of the verb *bestealcode*
J. *lēode, weras,* and *wīf* are direct objects of the verb *slōg*

2-7.
A. Answers will vary.
B. Among many possible observations, note the preference for straight lines, and for angles rather than curves. Runes would have been easier to carve into stone than curved letters would be. But not necessarily easier to carve into wood or

other materials with a marked grain. You may note the striking similarities to Roman letters like R, I, H, B, and M; you may notice as well that some other runes are very close to Roman letters (T, S). But while those similarities may suggest contact and influence, it is not clear that these similarities provide evidence for a common origin.

2-8.

A. Ælfric argues that the English translation should not add anything to the Latin and should not change the order in which the Latin words occur. Note that this approach could cause certain problems, because the structure of Latin is not identical to the structure of Old English. Latin had, for example, inflection for the verb in the passive, but Old English formed the passive periphrastically (as does PDE), with *be* + the past participle. To translate a Latin passive into Old English, you must add a word, because Old English does not have a passive inflection for the verb. Ælfric does make allowances for accounting such differences when he adds that Latin and English are not the same sometimes: "do not have one and the same way in the experiencing of speech." But you can see that despite this reasonable allowance, Ælfric also emphasizes the primacy of the Latin version (not that the Latin version was *the* original!) over the Old English.

B. Ælfric is explicit that we should not change the order in which words occur unless it is necessary given the rules of Old English. That statement is complex: it suggests that word order may be recognized as literally and rhetorically significant, but it also may suggest that word order is also recognized as potentially grammatically significant as well.

C. For Ælfric, word order must be changed when the rules of Old English require that change for grammaticality and sense. But we should pay attention to the fact that Ælfric explains that this change is necessary only because not everyone who reads the translation also knows Latin. That means his translation is not intended for a bilingual audience alone.

D. Ælfric follows his discussion of translation immediately with an argument for the importance of both the Old and the New Testaments, and he naturalizes the argument by suggesting that having two testaments is like having two lips, two eyes, two ears, etc. So the idea of having two versions of two testaments (one Latin and one Old English) can be subsumed into the logic of his later argument.

PART THREE: ADVANCED EXERCISES

3-1.

A. *cnapan* (weak noun, masculine genitive singular)

B. *widuwan* (weak noun, feminine genitive singular)

C. *earm* (strong noun, masculine nominative singular)

D. *earm* (strong noun, masculine nominative singular)

E. *se* (masculine nominative singular)

F. *meolce* (strong noun, feminine dative singular)

G. *hātre* (strong feminine dative singular)

H. ġif cnapan earm tōbrocen sīe, ġenim þā wyrte betonican, þiġe hīe þonne on hātre meolce. Þonne hālað se earm swyðe hraðe.

3-2.

A. mann/hund/huntan/cnapan (masculine, singular accusative): note that because þone is a masculine singular accusative form, it will agree with a masculine singular accusative noun. The masculine nouns above are *mann, cnapa, hund,* and *hunta.* Their singular accusative forms are *mann, cnapan, hund,* and *huntan* Any of those forms would be correct.

B. hund/earm/hunta/cnapa/mann (masculine nominative singular); wīf/bēor/hēafod (neuter accusative singular); hunde/earme/huntan/cnapan/menn/bēore/wīfe (masculine or neuter dative singular: note that while the OE form þǣm can be singular or plural, the PDE *that* can only be singular)

C. wīf/hēafod/bēor (neuter nominative singular); hund/earm/huntan/cnapan/mann (masculine accusative singular); lāre/widuwan/nǣdran (feminine dative singular)

D. lār/widuwe/nǣdre (feminine nominative singular)

E. hund/earm/hunta/cnapa/mann (masculine nominative singular)

F. hundes/earmes/huntan/cnapan/mannes/bēores/wīfes/hēafodes (masculine or neuter genitive singular)

G. lāre/widuwan/nǣdran (feminine genitive singular)

H. wīf/bēor/hēafod (neuter accusative singular)

I. lāre/widuwan/nǣdran (feminine accusative singular: note that while the OE form þā can be feminine accusative singular or all genders nominative or accusative plural, in this sentence, with Iċ as the subject, it must be accusative, and the PDE *that* means it must also be singular)

J. hund/earm/hunta/cnapa/mann (masculine nominative singular); hund/earm/huntan/cnapan/mann (masculine accusative singular)

K. lār/widuwe/nǣdre (feminine nominative singular); wīf/bēor/hēafod (neuter accusative singular)

3-3.

A. nominative; genitive or dative/The dragon set his mouth over the head of the holy woman
B. accusative/and swallowed her
C. nominative/The holy Margaret made the sign of Christ
D. genitive/inside the belly of the dragon
E. nominative; accusative/she split him into two parts
F. nominative/and the holy woman went out of the belly of the dragon unstained
G. nominative/and the devil rose up
H. accusative; dative/The holy Margaret grasped the devil by the lock (of hair)
I. accusative/And cast him onto the earth
J. genitive/and put out his right eye
K. genitive/and burst all his bones and set her foot over his neck
L. dative/and said to him: "Get away from my maidenhood!"

3-4.

A. swīcan; swicon; swicen
B. hrīnan; hrān; hrinen
C. snāþ; sniþon; sniþen
D. stīgan; stāg; stigon
E. scufon; scofen
F. lēat; luton; loten
G. smēac; smucon
H. hrēaw; hrowen
I. 1st
J. 1st
K. 2nd
L. 2nd
M. Class 1 strong verb
N. Class 1 strong verb
O. Class 1 strong verb
P. Class 2 strong verb
Q. Class 1 strong verb
R. Class 1 strong verb
S. weak

3-5.

A. SV
B. VS
C. þā SV → *when* (subordinate conjuction); þā VS → *then* (adverb)
D. Answers will vary. One reason we might find this pattern more frequently in texts translated from Latin is that Old English does not use hypotaxis and subordination as extensively as Latin does; this structure may reflect an effort to carry some of the Latin hypotaxis into the OE translation. Some of the poetry we have in OE is clearly not translated from Latin. One reason we do not find this structure in the poetry may have to do with the more paratactic styles associated with native poetry.

3-6.

A. All of the words practiced here are found below, in the passage to be transliterated for the next item.

B. ðonne is oðer ealand suð fram brixonte/ on þam beoð menn akende butan heaf/ dum þa habbaþ on breostum heora/ eagan and muð hi syndon eahta fota longe/ and eahta fota brade

C. beoð buton/ heafdum þa habbað/ on hyra breostum/ heora eagan and muð/ seondon eahta/ fota lange and eahta/ fota brade

D. Answers may vary but might include reference to the elaborate and ornate illustrations in the Tiberius Bv version, and the very different style in the Vitellius Axv version as well as to the partial or absent frames in the Vitellius Axv version as opposed to the careful framing in the Tiberius Bv version. Another point to note is that the Tiberius Bv version is very tidy, clear, and legible, in its measured columns, in contrast to the unpredictable layout of the text and images in the Vitellius Axv version.

E. Answers will vary. One possible response involves the effect of the partial/absent frames: given that these are descriptions of fabulous creatures in the faraway East, the fact that in the Vitellius Axv version the frames do not seem to contain the creatures depicted may make those creatures seem more proximate, less contained, and distant from the viewer. But you might also notice that even in the Tiberius Bv version, the man with no head has his hands around the frame and is stepping on it. From another perspective, in the Tiberius Bv version, the Latin text comes first, above the Old English, and perhaps that may suggest a positioning of the two languages ideologically.

F. Yes! The bilingual version is open to an audience that knows Latin, as well as one that knows OE, as well as one that perhaps cannot read at all and so is concerned solely with the images. The monolingual version is only in the *native* language and in images, which may suggest a less scholarly audience and, perhaps, given the absence of the Latin text, one also less Rome-identified.

G. Answers will vary. One response might be that both versions address an audience that may not be literate.

Chapter Eight

1-1.

A. out

B. strength

C. at

D. sap

E. bath

F. right

G. thing

H. thou

I. hedge

J. teeth

K. light

L. chin

M. chest

N. foul

O. shrift

P. shilling

Q. childish

R. floor

S. wedge

T. sour

U. quick

1-2.

A. runge

B. nute (nut)

C. nekke (neck)

D. rok (rock)

E. hed (head)

F. lavedi; lady (lady)

G. loverd; lord (lord)

H. eche (each)

I. suche (such)

J. wenche (wench)

K. much (much)

1-3.

A. tunga (-n > Ø); tunge (-a > -ə> Ø)

B. name (-a > -ə > Ø)

C. nama (-n > Ø); name (-a > -ə > Ø)

D. nama (-n > Ø); name (-a > -ǝ > Ø)

E. nama (-n > Ø); name (-a > -ǝ > Ø)

F. nama (-n > Ø); name (-a > -ǝ > Ø)

G. namen (-a > -ǝ > Ø); name (-n > Ø); name (-e >-ǝ > Ø)

H. namun (-m > -n); namu (-n > Ø); name (-u > -ǝ > Ø)

I. nama (-n > Ø); name (-a > -ǝ > Ø)

J. heall

K. heall (-e > -ǝ > Ø)

L. heall (-e > -ǝ > Ø)

M. heall (-e > -ǝ > Ø)

N. heall (-a > -ǝ > Ø)

O. heallen (-a > -ǝ > Ø); healle (-n > Ø); heall (-e >-ǝ > Ø)

P. heallun (-m > -n); heallu (-n > Ø); heall (-u > -ǝ > Ø)

Q. heall (-a > -ǝ > Ø)

R. One form for each word

S. names and halls; name's and hall's

T. gāst

U. gāstes

V. gāst (-e > -ǝ > Ø)

W. gāst

X. gāstas

Y. gāst (-a > -ǝ > Ø)

Z. gāstun (-m > -n); gāstu (-n > Ø); gāst (-a > -ǝ > Ø)

AA. gāstas

BB. Three (gāst, gāstes, gāstas)

CC. The genitive singular and nominative/accusative plural forms from the strong masculine nouns in OE.

1-4. A. Answers will vary, but in most instances, predicted words in this category will be predominantly borrowings, and usually from French in the later ME period; B. answers will vary and should generate some examination of which words are native and which borrowed, usually from French in the later ME period.

1-5.

A. 3

B. 7

C. 6

D. 5

E. 1

F. 2

G. 4

1-6.

A. ---

B. Answers will vary but we count 12 for our own printing

C. ---

D. Answers may vary. Likely observations include fewer pen lifts, rounder and connected letters

E. yes

F. ---

G. once

PART TWO: INTERMEDIATE EXERCISES

2-1.

A. spi<u>ndl</u>e

B. thu<u>ndr</u>e

C. e<u>mpt</u>y

D. behe<u>st</u>

E. auncie<u>nt</u>

F. tyrau<u>nt</u>

G. bre<u>mbl</u>e

H. thi<u>mbl</u>e

I. tu<u>mbl</u>er

J. thu<u>mb</u>

2-2.

A. <th>; <ou>; <ee>

B. /ɑ/; Ø; -ə > Ø

C. -s for plural

D. SV

E. thee

F. water; cume

G. water

H. SV (Peter answered)

I. <th>; <oo>

J. /ɑ/; r

K. "of" genitive; splits to demonstrative *that* and invariable definite article *the*

L. SV

M. that; roof

N. was

O. of the ark; of the earth

P. Noah opened

2-3.

A. Northern

B. Northern

C. Southern

D. Southern

E. Northern

2-4.

A. 1. Norman Conquest

2. Start of the Hundred Years' War because the Hundred Years' War is waged in part as a *result* of the complicated dynastic and political entanglements between England and France that occurred when the Duke of Normandy became *both* the King of England and the Duke of Normandy.

B. 1. Start of the Hundred Years' War

2. English Peasants' Revolt because one of the immediate causes of the Revolt was a poll tax to fund the ongoing Hundred Years' War.

C. 1. Marriage of Æthelred and Emma

2. Norman Conquest because one of the claims to the throne of England after the death of Æthelred that William the Conquerer had was his blood relation to Emma.

D. 1. Rule of the Danish kings

2. Norman Conquest because during the rule of the Danish kings, the exiled Wessex line continued to build contacts in Normandy; also because during the rule of the Danish kings, the origins of the treaty that gave Harald Haardrada the claim to the throne of English (part of the motivation for the Norwegian attack in 1066) are set in place.

E. 1. Rule of the Danish kings

2. English victory at Stamford Bridge because during the rule of the Danish kings the origins of the treaty that gave Harald Haardrada the claim to the throne of England (and part of his motivation to invade) were set in place.

F. 1. Black Plague

2. English Peasants' Revolt because the Peasants' Revolt is also partly motivated by the increase in economic power and geographic and social mobility afforded to "Those Who Work" as a result of the labor shortages following the Black Plague.

PART THREE: ADVANCED EXERCISES

3-1.

A. þe (line 1); te (line 3); þ- (that is as a prefix on the word *emperice* in line 5)

B. scae; [ʃæ]

C. hi

D. athas (line 5); strengthe (line 10); wurthen (line 13); the digraph here appears inside words, whereas <þ> and <ð> appear at the beginning of words

E. –en

F. –en

G. Answers may vary, but should include some observations about the behavior of the possessive -*s*, that unlike other inflectional suffixes, it can attach to the last word of a phrase or clause, like a clitic (as in *King Henry's nose*, but also *the King of England's nose*, or *the man I love's nose*). Clitics are treated more fully in Chapter Ten of the textbook and the workbook.

3-2.

A. [d] is a voiced alveolar stop; [n] is a voiced alveolar nasal; [r] is a voiced alveolar trill[1]
B. [p] is a voiceless bilabial stop; [m] is a voiced bilabial nasal; [t] is a voiceless alveolar stop
C. [b] is a voiced bilabial stop; [m] is a voiced bilabial nasal; [l] is a voiced alveolar lateral
D. the insertion of a sound, called epenthesis, which occurs because of the perception of a sound as articulation moves from one place to another or one manner to another

3-3.

A. -s in *has*, line 1; -s in *boes*, line 2; -s in *gas*, line 12; -s in *wagges*, line 14; -s in *falles*, line 17
B. -s in *werkes*, line 5
C. *is*, line 6 and line 20
D. *na*, line 1; *ham*, line 7; *gas*, line 12; *fra*, line 14; *swa*, line 15
E. -th in *gooth*, line 12; -th in *looketh*, line 14; -th in *hath*, line 14; -th in *goth*, line 17; -th in *strepeth*, line 18
F. -e or Ø in *wene*, line 3; -e or Ø in *make*, line 6
G. subject form is *they*, line 3, line 6; possessive form is *hir*, line 1, line 4, line 5, line 11; object form is *hem*, line 3, line 8

3-4. Answers to questions A through I can be verified with reference to the image in the workbook. J. Answers may vary but likely responses are <b, c, e, g, k, l, m, n, o, p, u> K and L. Writing individual letters, minim by minim, can encourage letter-by-letter copying. Longer segments require scribes to hold a syllable or word, or even a phrase in mind while copying. Longer segments thus might facilitate shifting from what is in the source text to the sounds of the scribe's own variety of English.

---

1 The actual quality of /r/ in Middle English is not sure and surely varied by region. Here we represent it as [r], which in IPA is normally used to indicate a voiced alveolar trill. It may have been a tap or even a liquid, as it is in most varieties of Modern English, however.

3-5. Answers may vary for all of these items.

A. Latin remained the language of scholarship, but the tradition of courtly love first emerges in French. Here the movement between Anglo-Norman and Latin underscores the close relationship between the two languages but also marks this poem as scholarly or at least learned, evoking the language of the Church as well, even in this secular context.

B. Being an English student meant literacy in Latin, French, and English. That literacy could link an English student's intellectual life to intellectual communities across Europe, in which literacy in French and Latin was also required. Here the student in fact informs us, in French, that he lives in France.

C. The shift in the final two lines of the poem to Middle English is dramatic here, signaling perhaps a departure from convention into a more heartfelt longing (of course also conventional).

D. Because of the required literacy in French, Latin, and English (at least) for students and scholars during the Middle English period, some linguistic awareness of echoes across languages, and of cross-linguistic resonances, surely existed and informed literary choices. Although most of us have to look these things up, it is not a stretch to suggest that highly literate audiences in the ME period might have recognized them. Here, reading "duel" across the three languages in this poem might support an interpretation of the love-longing suffered by the student/poet as also, self-consciously, love-longing created by a literary tradition he perpetuates. But surely you have other ideas as well!

Chapter Nine

PART ONE: BEGINNING EXERCISES

1-1.

A. see; sea

B. we; wee

C. rote; wrote

D. met

E. I; ay; eye

F. flour; flower

G. town

H. ate; eight

I. at

J. fate

K. feet; feat

L. mode; mowed

M. mood; mooed

N. soon

O. so; sow; sew

P. tote

Q. tap

R. tape

S. box

T. ox

U. [i]

V. [e]

W. [u]

X. [o]

Y. [ɑi]

Z. [ɑu]

AA. [æ]

BB. [ɑ]

CC. [ɔ]

DD. [i]

EE. set

FF. cape

GG. Pa

HH. bone

II. wheat

JJ. toot

KK. bite

LL. cloud

MM. cats

NN. we

OO. ɑi; i; i; e; ɑu; u; e; o

1-2.

A. Gawain

B. He is being both familiar and insulting.

C. Lancelot

D. He is being scrupulously polite. He is trying to avoid a conflict he knows will be disastrous.

E. *You* is plural here. Gawain is referring to Lancelot and Guenevere together.

F. Lancelot seems a little angry here!

1-3.

A. dare; work

B. Answers may vary, but will most likely include: shine; slay; thrive; burst; cling; fling; strive

1-4.

A. present passive

B. past passive

C. present active perfect

D. past passive perfect

E. future active

F. future passive

G. I do not love.

H. Do I love?

I. What do you love?

1-5. Answers will vary.

PART TWO: INTERMEDIATE EXERCISES

2-1.

A. [i] yes

B. [e] not fully

C. [i] yes

D. [e] not fully

E. [e] not fully

F. [o] yes

G. [o] yes

H. [ɔ] no

I. [o] yes

2-2. A. frequency

2-3. Answers to all of the items in this section may vary.

A. One effect of standardization of spelling is the idea that there is a "true writing," or a "true" way to spell a word, and hence that other spellings must be wrong and "false," even if they more closely approximate the sounds of a word. Another is that this "true" spelling must be learned: it is not simply intuitive given a basic knowledge of a set of symbols and the sounds they represent.

B. "Ladies, Gentlewomen, or any other unskillful persons"

C. That such a reference might be directed to women readers suggests that there is a reading audience of women who might purchase and use it. Also that using language "properly" is becoming part of what it means to be "ladies" or "gentlewomen."

D. The first reason presented is that the book will help them to read and understand Scripture. This makes clear the assumption that many people are actually reading Scripture, a new phenomenon in the early Modern period. But the usefulness of the book is also proposed to be in aiding understanding of what is heard or read "elsewhere" and in actively employing the same words. This suggests that "hard words" are part of daily life, not just scholarly jargon.

E. Perhaps because the point of the book is to make "hard words" accessible to "unskillful persons." Providing both the Latin and the translation demonstrates the author's knowledge of the Latin at the same time that it promises access to some of that knowledge to its readers.

F. Here the use of the word "aptly" suggests prescription, the idea that there is a "right" way to use a word. Learning that "right" way is only partly about fluency in the language itself.

G. While alphabetic glosses can be dated to long before the early Modern English period, the organization of words here also establishes the usability of this book as a reference, and the idea that words can be looked up if you don't know what they mean or how to use them: this is a new concept emerging in this period.

PART THREE: ADVANCED EXERCISES

3-1.

A. [ɛ]; [i]; [e]; [i]; [ɛ]; [i] Here, as in the example, we might consider that [ɛ] likely shifted to [i] later than some of the other vowels in the GVS, and that in this sample, from 1596, it seems most probable that if these words actually rhymed, they did so because the vowels in *feare, heat,* and *beat* most clearly had not yet shifted all the way to [i].

B. [i]; [ɑi]; [ɑi]; [i]; [ɑi]; [i]; [ɑi]; [i] The final sounds in *prophecies, history,* and *jealousy* were likely [i] in Shakespeare's time. The vowel in the word *eye* in ME was closer to [e]. It seems likely, then, that here we can see that the [e] of *eye* may have shifted to [i], but not yet to its PDE pronunciation of [ɑi].

C. [i]; [ɛ]; [e]; [i] As in Item A above, it seems most probable that if these words rhymed, it was because the vowel in *meat* had not yet shifted fully to [i].

D. Answers will vary. Some considerations include the problem that the word *eye* probably had a vowel closer to [e] in ME, and while it likely shifted during the GVS to [i] it also will shift further to [ɑi] in many varieties of English. The word *symmetry* is very like those words ending in -y encountered earlier in this exercise. One possible reading of this rhyme is that it reflects the pronunciation of a variety of English in which *eye* was still pronounced [i]. Another possible reading requires that we consider the literary history of these rhymes, from times when actual rhymes were more likely: it is certainly possible that these words rhymed *on the page* because of the significance of figures like Shakespeare who wrote when those words might have rhymed in actual usage. In other words later writers may have imitated earlier rhymes in an attempt to lend solemnity or apparent erudition to their texts.

3-2.

A. (2)
B. (3)
C. (5)
D. (6)
E. (7)
F. (9)

G. (8)
H. (11)
I. (10)
J. (12)
K. (1)
L. (4)

3-3.

A. yes, yes, yes, yes, yes
B. no, no, no, no, yes
C. no, no, no, no, yes
D. yes, yes, yes, yes, yes
E. yes, yes, yes, yes, yes

(It is difficult for us to determine without more research what classes of words *'ve* does attach to.)

3-4.

A. One reason is that we tend to have SVO as a pattern, even though here we have a copula, which does not take an object.

B. *Than* can be a preposition or a subordinate conjunction. When it is a preposition it will take an object form of the pronoun. When it is a subordinate conjunction, we expect both a subject and a verb to follow it. We choose *me* for *She is older than me* because in this context we understand *than* as a preposition. The prescription requires us to assume that a clause should follow and that *I* is the subject in a sort of reduced version of that clause.

C. Because infinitives in PDE are periphrastic we *can* split infinitives and doing so sometimes allows us to put words, such as adverbs, right before the verb, making the use of such expressions unambiguous and perhaps more forceful.

D. One reason has to do with the plural sense of the phrase *each student*. While *each* implies that we are talking about a single student, the sense is plural, and for that reason we may chose *their*. In the present moment, however, many people are uncomfortable with a default masculine pronoun for a phrase like *each student*, and equally so with chosing *her*, or *his or her*. Furthermore, cultural discomfort with assumptions about gender has also motivated the use of "they/their/them" with a singular meaning.

E. Hypercorrection. When the pronoun *I* is used as part of a compound subject (*Jacinto and I had dinner*), *I* is supposed to come last. Furthermore, although sentences like *Me and Jacinto had dinner* will certainly be uttered by speakers of English, *I* is the subject form. The "rule" to avoid *me* in this context, and to place *I* last in a compound subject, is one, like "don't end a sentence with a preposition," that is actively taught in grammar schools. The prescribed pattern "X and I" is extended to other contexts, especially when speakers are aiming to be "correct."

3-5.

A. -s
B. politeness
C. it is lost
D. -eth
E. thou
F. -est
G. Intentional archaism

3-6.

A. man, us
B. man, seat
C. ---
D. that, Shepherd
E. who, Seed, how the Heav'ns and Earth / Rose out of Chaos
F. Heav'ns, Earth
G. Sion Hill, Siloa's Brook, thee
H. that
I. I, aid
J. that

K. it, things
L. *whose mortal taste / Brought Death into the World...Seat* modifies *Tree*
M. *that on the secret top of Oreb, or of Sinae didst inspire / That Shepherd...Chaos* modifies *Muse*
N. *who first taught the chosen Seed...Chaos* modifies *Shepherd*
O. *that flow'd Fast by the Oracle of God* modifies *Siloa's Brook*
P. *That with no middle flight intends to soar...Mount* modifies *Song*
Q. *Sing; I invoke aid*
R. Answers will vary. Some considerations include the intentional slowing down of reading, requiring constant retracing and backtracking, significant because Milton is writing an epic on the Fall of Man, retracing and backtracking to moments of originary transgression; in addition, Milton's evocation of the language of other epics, written in languages with highly developed strategies of hypotaxis and subordination, such as Virgil's *Aeneid*.

3-7. Answers will vary. Arguments for the introduction of a neologism may involve creating a word for a concept that has not yet existed, or for creating a "fancier" word or a euphemism for a term that already exists. In the case of the latter, however, you should be very clear about why the Latinate neologism is necessarily "fancier" or more polite or more precise than what might be available in the existing lexicon. Accessing that logic should make clear the assumptions about Classical languages and the lexicon of English that still persist!

Chapter Ten

PART ONE: BEGINNER EXERCISES

1-1.
A. Outer
B. Inner
C. Expanding
D. Expanding
E. Inner
F. Outer

1-2.
A. hi, wi
B. shi, im
C. wi, it
D. i, im
E. yu, dem
F. shi, shi
G. a, it
H. de, mi
I. wi, dem,
J. yu, it

1-3.
A. [ðaɹ]
B. [teint]
C. [æn]
D. [lon]
E. [sɛtəlmɪnt]
F. [sɛtʃ]
G. [ɛz] or [ɪz]
H. [jə]

I. [kɪn]
J. [hɛv]
K. [tə]
L. [fr̩]
M. [ɔrə]
N. [gɪt]
O. [ɛɹ]

(Note that it may occur to you that some of these are just odd spellings but do not necessarily represent pronununciations different from Standard English. The practice of providing variant spellings, but not necessarily variant pronunciations, is a practice generally known as "eye-dialect," which is taken up later in this chapter.)

PART TWO: INTERMEDIATE EXERCISES

2-1.

A. [t] and [tʃ]

B. [d] and [dʒ]

C. [s] and [ʃ]

D. [z] and [ʒ]

E. palatalization

F. [u]

2-2.

A. they have only two forms

B. the simple past takes the form of the past participle, and the past participle takes the form of the simple past; in the set of simple past to past participle are *bring, brung, brung; do, done, done; drink, drunk, drunk; ring, rung, rung; stink, stunk, stunk; swim, swum, swum*; in the set of past participle to simple past are *bite, bit, bit; blow, blew, blew; break, broke, broke; choose, chose, chose; shake, shook, shook; take, took, took; tear, tore, tore; wake, woke, woke*

C. *catch, grow, know, teach*

2-3.

A. be, will, have; modal auxiliaries and do

B. 'll no; couldnae; 're no; shouldnae; mustnae

2-4.

A. Ed Joyce is after announcing his retirement...

B. Taoiseach Leo Varadkar said a Yes vote in Friday's referendum on the Eighth Amendment can help lift the stigma for 170,000 women who are after travelling abroad to seek a termination...

C. We are after increasing the number...

D. The woman is after being charged...

E. The proposal is after gathering momentum...

PART THREE: ADVANCED EXERCISES

3-1.

A. Although Canada clearly falls into the designation "inner circle," that descriptor elides the significance of the official status of French as well as a number of Indigenous languages on a regional level, as well as the presence of a vast number of other Indigenous languages.

B. Although English is one of the twelve official languages, and the de facto language for most federal functions in South Africa, describing English in South Africa as an "inner circle" language does not reflect the linguistic situation, in which English speakers are not the majority, in which many other languages have official status, and in which many, many other languages are spoken. But English in South Africa is not an "outer circle" language, either: it is a native language for about a quarter of the population.

C. Because English is not the official language of New Zealand, New Zealand would not fall into the "inner circle" designation. But because the official language, Maori, is spoken by such a small percentage of the population, whereas English is spoken by the majority of the population, the linguistic situatedness of English in New Zealand seems much closer to that of an "inner circle" than that of an "outer circle" country.

3-2.

A. This map distributes areas of representation according to population, and in that way prioritizes population over territory. The largest areas of the map are granted to the countries with the largest populations. This map suggests that power or shares in control of the world may have to do with the numbers of people in a country rather than the quantity of land that country controls.

B. This map positions the southern hemisphere at the top of the map. There is no reason other than ideology for placing north at the top of maps. Recall from the textbook that early maps like the T-O maps placed east at the top. Inverting the now conventional perspective suggests that the dominance of the northern hemisphere is not "natural" or simply the way the world is. On the contrary, it reflects a way of seeing the world that was created and reinforced during the period of European "expansion."

C. This map shows the world with certain countries marked out as being a high security risk or a low security risk. The map is clearly intended for an American or Western European audience and by presenting security in such binary and unexplained terms supports the stereotypes of certain countries and their inhabitants as inherently dangerous.

D. This map assigns the expression for "thank you" in some languages of the world, set in their (approximate) geographical locations by country or continent. Since the size of the word presumably corresponds, although not accurately, to the number of speakers of the various languages the map represents, it can be thought of as being similar to the population map in suggesting that shares in control of the world may be understood in terms of number of speakers of a language rather than territory. Obviously too the map cannot represent all 7,000 or so languages of the world, assuming even that there is an equivalent of "thank you" in every language, which there almost certainly is not.

3-3. Answers may vary for both items in this section.
A. A few points that might emerge in the discussion: (1) often creoles develop in situations of economic oppression or even slavery, in which speakers are denied access to standard varieties of a lexifier language; (2) creoles develop much faster than do languages descended from a parent under more stable socio-cultural conditions.
B. One reason may have to do with difficulty in tracing all of the languages that may contribute to a pidgin/creole. But more fundamentally, the genealogical metaphor does not have the flexibility to account for the development of languages with multiple sources, and for which the lexifier language cannot be considered the sole "parent." It has also been suggested that creole languages lack input of any parent language and therefore revert to some kind of "natural" human grammar.

3-4.
A. regional: *somepin, fin', ever'*; eye dialect: *doin', jus', bein', tryin', comin', an'*
B. Yes, for example, why isn't the *'t* deleted on *don't*? Why is the preposition and infinitival marker *to* always in its full and unreduced form?
C. Yes, and in fact most of these pronunciations would be used by all English speakers in casual, unregulated speech.

Image Sources

Page 47: Public domain image from Wikimedia Commons, creator ovi gainz.

Page 53: Public domain image from Wikimedia Commons, creator historicair.

Page 59: Public domain image from Wikimedia Commons, creator wooptoo.

Page 82: Public domain image from Wikimedia Commons. Original: Tsui – Derivative work: Curtis3250692~commonswiki + Maphobbyist.

Page 136: See page 138.

Page 137: See page 139.

Page 138: Cotton Tiberius f. 82r. Image courtesy of the British Library.

Page 139: Cotton MS Vitellius A XV, f. 102v. Image courtesy of the British Library.

Page 167: Harley 2253, f.55v. Image courtesy of the British Library.

Page 183: Title page of *A Table Alphabeticall* by Robert Cawdry, 1613.

Page 193: Psalm 23 from the 1611 edition of the King James Bible.

Page 211: Population Map. Copyright © 2015, www.ManyWaysToSeeTheWorld.org. Published by ODTmaps, Amherst, MA; phone 413-549-1293; email ODTstore@ odt.org. Reprinted by permission.

Page 212 top: © Shutterstock/Pyty.

Page 212 bottom: Security Risk Map, from MAPS: 4 Different Ways of Looking at Risk in the World, by Elena Holodny. As seen at https://www.businessinsider.com/ eiu-global-risks-maps-2015-8.

Page 213: © Shutterstock/dizain.

From the Publisher

A name never says it all, but the word "Broadview" expresses a good deal of the philosophy behind our company. We are open to a broad range of academic approaches and political viewpoints. We pay attention to the broad impact book publishing and book printing has in the wider world; for some years now we have used 100% recycled paper for most titles. Our publishing program is internationally oriented and broad-ranging. Our individual titles often appeal to a broad readership too; many are of interest as much to general readers as to academics and students.

Founded in 1985, Broadview remains a fully independent company owned by its shareholders—not an imprint or subsidiary of a larger multinational.

For the most accurate information on our books (including information on pricing, editions, and formats) please visit our website at www.broadviewpress.com. Our print books and ebooks are also available for sale on our site.

broadview press
www.broadviewpress.com